THE
VIDEO EDITING
HANDBOOK

for beginners

By Aaron Goold

License Notes

VIDEO LINKS

This book comes with some very helpful video demonstrations.

To view the videos that accompany many of these sections visit...

https://videoeditinghandbook.com/videos-e2

...and find the video of the same title.

I'll update these videos frequently and add new videos throughout the lifetime of this edition. If you have any problems accessing the videos, feel free to contact me:

videoeditinghandbook.com/support

TABLE OF CONTENT

WHY A BOOK ON VIDEO EDITING?

A follow-up question to the title of this chapter might be... "Why not a YouTube channel instead? Or a website with articles?"

First, I like books, especially hard copies. I'm used to learning from books and appreciate them as a medium. They don't require batteries, don't have annoying pop-ups (except children's books), are easier on the eyes for some people, and, most importantly, they effectively package ideas, sometimes for thousands of years. We can revisit and compare success rates between books and YouTube playlists in the year 3000 if you like.

Of course, some topics benefit from a different medium. Video obviously benefits from its own medium, video. Nothing stopped me from publishing both books and videos, so that's what I did: I offered this book as well a long list of videos (see the previous section for the link).

In these videos, I show you how to do things. I explain ideas as if you were sitting next to me. That kind of relationship has value, but so does studying alone with a book, a book carefully written to follow a structure and logic that real-time, impromptu lessons don't always provide.

And as much as I love videos and movies, they are relatively ephemeral, especially videos today. Books can be forgotten, but paper books don't disappear just because someone forgot to pay the web server invoice or because your kid put a magnet on the hard drive. Books are tough and they'll get you through almost anything, even editing videos.

QUICKSTART

I just told you how much I love books and believe even video editing is worthy of a book. So it only makes sense that the first thing I ask of you is... to watch a video.

But it's true. You'll benefit from this book by frequently switching over to the videos. If you've ever learned a language from a book with a CD or audio supplement, treat this book the same. You'll gain the most understanding by first reading, then watching, then doing.

For this Quickstart, the installation details are simple, but sometimes tedious and change every few months. In the video I'll show you how to install Premiere Pro as well as the Adobe Creative Cloud, my preferred editing software. But I will also navigate to a few other editor homepages and explain what to expect when you download and install these other options as well.

This chapter is for those of you who are impatient, like me, and want to get working as quickly as possible. For those of you who are not yet convinced you need or want Premiere Pro, you can just watch the video to get a sense of the entire editing process.

I will show you the installation of Premiere, a brief overview of how it works, how to use it, and what to do when you're done editing. This chapter is also for those of you who are not only completely new to video editing but also unfamiliar with many of the computer skills commonly associated with handling video. If you feel you have a solid understanding of basic video and computer concepts, by all means, skip to the rest of the book.

HOW TO USE THIS BOOK

Besides using the videos on the website, you'll benefit from a few more notes about this book.

Practical

I intend this book for building practical videos, videos such as commercials, tutorials, lectures, informationals, events, and vlogs. These are videos that, ultimately, point the viewer towards something else -- a product, an idea. Practical videos use a different strategy than cinema. The "rules" are different. You might find some crossover between this and a cinema theory book, but for the most part, this is closer to a marketing book than an art book.

Beginner

This is also meant for the individual newbie, especially for those who need video for a business or project, but can't afford a full-time or experienced video specialist. If you are familiar with making basic videos, you'll benefit more from the details of the how and why we do something. If you've been editing for many years, this might be too basic of a book. But you also might be surprised...

Principles

The video market and tools change quickly. But many things do not change as quickly and some never change at all. I focus mostly on the unchanging, steady concepts in video, the principles. With these principles, you can choose whichever software or setup you like and still be productive. Learning how to do something special with a certain computer program is not as valuable as knowing *that* something special exists in the first place.

Website

I can't stress it enough: if you're not using the website, you're not getting the full book. As I write this, the website has only a few resources. But that is rapidly changing. The website will be your hub for new tools and updates and any other special features I decide to post.

Beyond video

You'll actually pick up more knowledge than just video. You'll learn some computer and internet stuff as well as marketing along the way. Most video positions require proficiency in all three categories: video, computers, marketing. This book will set you up for that career.

COMPUTERS AND SOFTWARE

For better and worse, we've transitioned from *film*making to *video*making. And instead of changing film canisters in black bags and squinting at 16mm reels in lamp light, we import video into another kind of black bag known as a computer. While you don't need an electrical engineering degree to get started in video, picking up imaging and hardware knowledge along the way will serve you well, especially if you plan to become a professional.

When you start editing simple videos you probably won't need to buy new computer stuff. Most computers manufactured in the last five years can handle **high-definition** video at 1,080 pixels. If the computer you are using was manufactured after 2017 and is not a low-powered machine like a Surface or Chromebook, it can likely playback and manipulate normal cell phone or DSLR video.

For cutting-edge video such as Ultra HD, 360, or stereoscopic, system and hardware requirements update much faster than they used to, so be prepared to buy new computers or parts every other year. The benefit of editing on a PC is changing the parts instead of the entire computer, as you will have to do with a Mac. You might be able to get away with a cheaper, older computer with some lightweight editing software for a small project. But eventually you will either hit a memory or CPU limit or just get frustrated with a weak system.

To edit general HD videos with limited effects and layers, the computer you require have these qualities:

- OS: Windows 10. Mac 10.14 (Mojave) or higher.

- **RAM:** Preferably more than 8 gigabytes. More than 16 gigabytes if you're going to get serious.

- Hard drive memory: At least 300 gigabytes of free space (SSD or disc drive are both fine for starting out).

- **Graphics card:** A GPU with at least 4 gigabytes of VRAM.

- **Processor:** Intel 7th Generation or newer. Or AMD equivalent (something like the Ryzen 7)

The requirements are always changing. But the software provider will usually list the above requirements on the web page. If not, search "hardware" or "software requirements for…" and the software you're interested in.

HOW MUCH COMPUTER STUFF DO I NEED TO KNOW?

In the beginning, it's not necessary to know all the details of how computer hardware works, but it won't hurt to start learning a little now. I cover most of the essential knowledge in this book. But understand: video software is not magic and it's not perfect. If your project is crashing, you will have to dig into the technical reasons as to why, get someone else to solve it, or use some preventative strategies that I explain in the section "Developing a System for Handling Problems".

RAW DEFINITION

A simple explanation of *raw* video is the binary data (the 1s and 0s) that the image sensor captures. Raw video is *unprocessed*. Most cellphones process the data created by the image sensor. Another way of putting it would be: cell phone cameras make the image look "better." Raw video uses no filters or adjustments.Raw images will look gray and flat. Many cameras provide contrast and saturation to the image file they save.

The raw capture process. The light of the scene goes into the camera. The camera saves the first impression of light.

The processed capture process. A second tool changes the original impression.

ULTRA HIGH DEFINITION

This refers to displays that are 16:9 in *aspect ratio* and have a minimum of 3840x2160 pixels. Many cell phones already record in Ultra HD and I expect Ultra will soon replace HD as the standard.

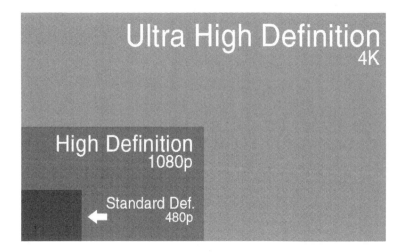

THE SOFTWARE YOU WILL NEED

Obviously you are going to need video editing software. Video editing software *imports* media from your computer hard drive or from an external hard drive. What is *media?* Media is anything that you are able to edit, primarily video, audio, music, and images. The editing software allows you to move the media around, save it, and *export* it. Each video editing software arranges media in its own distinct way, but all use the same basic tools to accomplish this arrangement. Here are some of the more common editing applications and which types of projects they're good for.

Adobe Premiere Pro

Premiere is made by the people at Adobe, the same company that owns Photoshop. I would recommend Premiere for more advanced editors or to anyone who knows he/she will be doing a lot of editing for a long time.

Advantages:

- It is easy to buy for both Mac and Windows operating systems.

- It is an affordable, comprehensive program. At this time, a subscription to Premiere on Adobe Creative Cloud is $21 a month. You get access to the Premiere program as well as a few other Adobe freebies.

- It functions well with all of the other Adobe software like Photoshop and After Effects.

- It will process any video an amateur or even a professional editor would require.

Disadvantages:

- It can be difficult for beginners to learn because it offers so many different features.

- It will at times crash or operate poorly depending on the model or age of your computer or the type of video files you're working with.

- It does require a bit of maintenance. For example: it will eat up much of your hard drive memory especially if you don't have a lot of memory to work with. See **Media caches eat up your hard drive space** in the *Stay Organized* chapter.

Adobe Rush

If you downloaded Premiere and were like "uhhh...." then you might want to try Rush first. It's a much simpler version of Premiere and ideal for projects like family videos, vlogs or single clips that just need to be trimmed and put in order. If you don't need a lot of media, effects, or robust audio options, then Rush might be the software to use. If you decide you need more editing tools, you can import your Rush project into Premiere.

The Rush creators publicize the software's use on mobile devices. That ability might come in handy if you want to make simple edits to cell phone videos and post to social media, but that's about all I'd recommend for mobile editing. The default iPhone video editor works just as well for most purposes, as do many standard Android galleries. But if you're serious about editing on your phone, Rush will give you just a few more features as well as integrate with the Adobe ecosystem.

Advantages:

- More affordable than Premiere

- Easier to learn

- Automated features for common needs (such as noise reduction)

- Requires fewer CPU resources

- Designed for mobile use

- Integrates with Premiere

Disadvantages:

- Limited features

- Consumes memory with video proxies (ie, smaller versions of your clips)

- Relies heavily on Creative Cloud connection

- Slower rendering than Premiere

Final Cut Pro

Final Cut Pro is Apple's video editing software. Final Cut Pro 7 at one time was the gold standard among serious and mid-level professional editors. Then Apple released Final Cut Pro X which removed several popular features. Many editors then were forced to use another program or continue to use the older version of Final Cut. Now Apple has done away with versioning (at least as far as the brand is concerned) and it's just called Final Cut. I can still recommend FC for either serious beginners or advanced editors because it has more than enough features and a large online community for troubleshooting and support.

Advantages:

- It has many convenient features.

- It is widely used by many professional and hobbyist editors.

- It requires only a one-time purchase so you will not continually be paying monthly subscriptions.

Disadvantages:

- It is for Macintosh computers only.

- It has a more expensive upfront fee: $300 at the Apple store at this time.

There are rumors Apple may discontinue the program. Even if that's *not* true, if the community of videomakers suspects a tool might not be available, they'll avoid using it.

Davinci Resolve by Blackmagic Design

In my opinion, Resolve is the only serious competitor for Premiere Pro in the general video editing market. A few years ago, Resolve was expensive and used only by professional color graders and finishers. Then Blackmagic decided to add a few more features and drop the price of Resolve to $300 (at the time of this publication). Resolve excels over Premiere in color grading and, in some ways, in audio mixing as well. The main drawback is that Resolve is not as easy to learn. You have to deal with a few more software details to setup and use Resolve.

Advantages:

- Top-notch color tools

- Node-based effect tools

- Supports complete project workflow (from assembly to audio mixing to rendering)

- Integrates well with Blackmagic imaging products

Disadvantages:

- Steep learning curve

- Requires more powerful hardware

- Not as "forgiving" nor supportive with media types as Premiere

Vegas by Magix

SONY used to release Vegas and for many years Vegas was a common platform, especially if you used SONY cameras. Vegas started as an audio program and still has many audio features that outperform the other video editors. However, the video editing community mostly favors Premiere, Davinci Resolve, or, occasionally, Final Cut X. If you plan to share your project or need help on something, Vegas will not integrate well with other software. Vegas still has more than enough features to get started in your editing endeavors and might be an option for those who don't want to pay the somewhat expensive Adobe subscription fee.

Advantages:

- Upfront payment (no subscription)

Disadvantages:

- Windows only

- Limited programs

- Declining popularity (but that's more my opinion)

Avid Media Composer

Avid Media Composer is owned by the company of the same name, Avid. It's the oldest of the major editing software programs and considered the most powerful. Most feature movies, TV shows and other extremely high-quality content are assembled on Avid. I would definitely NOT recommend Avid for a beginner or even an advanced editor. Unless you're working in a professional, fully equipped editing studio with a team, there is no reason to use Avid. It is better to begin your study of editing with a simpler program. Premiere, Final Cut or an alternative are better suited.

OTHER OPTIONS FOR BEGINNERS

iMovie

iMovie is Final Cut Pro's younger brother. It's an Apple-only program which is available to download for a $16 one-time fee from the Apple store. More recent Mac computers include iMovie for free.

In my career I have known many novice editors who got their start with iMovie. I highly recommend you give it a try as well.

Hitfilm by FXHome

FXhome'sHitFilm is a relatively new editor. Many reviewers describe HitFilm as a combination of Adobe's Premiere and After Effects, offering outstanding effects as well as general editing features. In fact, Hitfilm's interface looks similar to Premiere's, which makes switching between the two more comfortable. Most editors who require simple edits find the free version -- called Express -- meets all of their needs.

While Adobe uses a subscription service exclusively, HitFilm offers a "one-time fee" with options to update. If you download Express and decide you like it after a few days, you can always upgrade the Pro version.

Filmora

Filmora, which has been developed, by Wondershare is a subscription video editor considered by some users as popular and capable as the ones I have listed above. I have watched several tutorials but have never used it for any projects. The program has enough features for a beginner and for most hobbyist editors it may be all they will ever need. However, if you're going to spend anything more than $40 or anticipate becoming a professional editor, I suggest you consider buying Premiere or Premiere Rush.

Video Create, Adobe Spark, and Other Web-based Programs

Companies release video editors constantly now. Legacy companies such as Adobe are releasing different types of programs while other companies are fresh to the game, such as Vimeo. Most of the new programs are web-based, which means you don't have to download anything; you just use your web browser. This might work well for simple edits with video not larger than HD (1080 pixels), but web browsers are, so far, no replacement for dedicated desktop software. I write "currently" because I do anticipate that these web editor applications will improve as the server technology grows and browsers become more powerful. If you see a new web editor, it might be worthwhile to try it out. Someday one might replace the desktop editors.

GET ORGANIZED

FOLDERS AND BINS

Folders are on your computer. *Bins* are in your video software project. Both group and organize your data/media and should correlate with each other. The structures don't have to match perfectly, but should be very close. Here's an example:

```
Video Folder
---01_ProductionDocuments
---02_Raw
------Audio
------Misc
------Video
---03_Graphics
```

Caution about folders and professional cameras

Many high-end, professional cameras (like the RED or Canon C300) capture video differently from a cellphone or regular DSLR camera.

These cameras use specific names and folder structures for their videos and should never be changed unless you are an expert. This is because the clips and data reference each other by the names given by the camera. For organizing at a bin level within the video editing software and not your computer's folders, this is not a problem. In your editing software, you may change the name of the media and organize it without affecting the true name of the media in the computer's folder. It might look something like this:

```
CONTENTS
---CLIPS001
------AA2135
------AA2136
```

If you receive any video data that has a folder structure resembling the one above, talk to your producer, camera operator, or whomever shot the video. Ask that person which camera was used. You will then be able to search online for methods for importing and using it. For a more in depth example, find the video on website. Establish Naming Conventions

When you have only a handful of video clips, the clips can be named anything and you won't get confused. However, when you're working with hundreds of video files or creating many variations of the same video, deliberate naming of clips is essential for organization.

There is no rule for naming except consistency. Find a method that works and stick to it. Here's an example of what I consider good naming:

```
DAY_1_CAM_A_001.mov
(or) Day 1 - Camera A - 001 - Water
Splash.mov
```

I like this format because it tells me everything: which day (or session), which camera, and which order. Sometimes, depending on the project, I'll add descriptions at the end of the name (like in the second version). This is somewhat unusual in the editing world, although it works for me. Most editors recommend you put this information in the metadata.

Metadata is extra information included in your video or audio file. Some information, like date and time, is included automatically in the metadata. I also differ from many others in that I prefer underscores to hyphens (DAY-1-CAM-A-001.mov). Again, I have my reasons, but they're not really relevant in the scope of this book.

I've also heard never use the word "final," as in the final draft of something. I can see the purpose of this, because any video will rarely be final during a project. There are always some last-minute changes needed. With all that, I still use "final".

You might be pressured to "just start editing" and skip organizing. Sometimes you can't avoid this urgency, but you and the managers should understand that even though editing video is much more convenient than it used to be, it's still not magic. Good projects require that an editor be familiar with the content. Much of the editing is done in your brain before you edit a timeline and the first step to get the video in your head is to get organized.

Always be reviewing your content and media

Even though reviewing media and content overflows into the next chapter of this book, we can still use the process of organizing as an excellent opportunity to become familiar with the media with which we are working. Notice how many times a certain character or situation appears. Notice any patterns in camera movement. Also take notice which shots are completely useless and can be labeled as such. This is especially helpful for event videography like weddings, concerts, or anything with crowds. By the time you start making your selections you'll have a pretty good idea of content you have to work with.

THE EDITING TOOLBOX

You'll be happy to know that once you're organized, you're already fifty percent done with your project. Afterall, what's editing but a refinement of organization? Now we can finally play with the tools you'll use to put your video together. If you're using an editing program for the first time, I know what you're thinking: "Whoa, this is a lot of stuff on the screen." Don't worry. I'll show you only the most common and useful tools that are available in almost every major editing software. Before long, you'll be chopping video and moving it around no sweat.

The names and icons of the tools will be different for each editing program, but the functionality will be more or less the same. If you have questions, search online with "how to *do this thing* in *that program*." For example: "how to *unlink tracks in davinci resolve.*"

As a side note: All of these programs update and change frequently. Make it a habit to search for problems online and bookmark your favorite resources. At some point, you may have to ask a community forum your own question if you cannot find any answers. I have provided a list of useful forums and troubleshooting resources in Appendix: Resources.

Layout

The layout of an editing program is the placement of the panels of tools or media. Most editing programs have the following panels:

Project, Source Monitor, Program Monitor, Timeline, Tools, Effects and Other panels

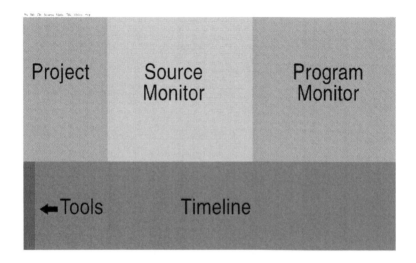

Project panel

The *project panel* is where your media will be. When you import audio or video or graphics, they will all sit in the project panel. The project panel is where all of your organized bins will be as well.

Source monitor

The source monitor is the place where you can view your unedited media. You can use the source monitor to mark media for notes or set in and out points--which is a way of editing the media--and add it to your timeline panel.

Program monitor

The *program monitor* is where you will see your editing. This is what the final product will be. In some programs (like Premiere and Final Cut) the program monitor also uses different displays and settings to help you see how the final video will look on different kinds of screens. It is not necessary to worry about those details for now, just understand that the program monitor is what you see when you play the timeline.

Which brings us to...

Timeline

The *timeline* is where you will spend most of your...well, time. However, that's not why it's called that. It's called the timeline because here you will see all of your media lined up and/or layered from beginning to end. The timeline is where you will make your cuts, add effects and line up media.

Effects and other panels

Each editing program has its own set of *effects, transitions* and other *tools*. Generally these extra tools will have their own panels or will be layered on top of each other inside a single panel. At the top of your program where it reads "File," "Edit," and all that, look for another option that reads "Window" (Final Cut, Premiere). If you don't see "Window" and are NOT using Premiere or Final Cut, search for "how to show panels in (name of your software)." From the "Window" drop down, you will see a list of panels. Check mark (or click) each panel that you would like to see.

I won't cover too many of these extra panels; just the basics for this book.

Importing media

Importing is the process of bringing media into your editing software. Most software allows you to drag and drop media into its project panel. I recommend that you use your program's built-in importing panel, assuming it has one.

Premiere, for example, has a **media browser** panel, which I introduced in the Quickstart chapter. From the media browser, you can search your computer for all of your videos, audio and graphics. Once you find it, you then choose "Import" from the media browser. I recommend importing media this way instead of drag and drop because it reduces errors.

As mentioned in the chapter on organization, some cameras use a complicated format to organize and save the video files onto the storage device like an SD card. If you were to drag and drop these video files into an editing program, you may notice some problems. If instead you use a tool like a *media browser* to import these video files, the program will read the video files properly. Video file types get complicated, so just know that importing video via the media browser or your software's equivalent is the safest method.

Bins

I wrote about bins in Get Organized, but to review, bins are the folders which reside inside your editing software.

Media

Media is a term which is used for any video, audio or graphic file you add to your project. I sometimes use the word *clip*. Clip usually means an edited file on your timeline. However, most people use these terms interchangeably.

Once you import your media into the editing program, you can change its name to whatever you want. The original file's name will not change. However, you might want to consider a naming structure for your project. You can be more flexible with media names than you can with folders and bins. It might be better to think of names in terms of how you'll use the media.

Here's an example: you and a friend have recorded a wedding. Each of you used a different camera. You were in charge of recording the main events, like the close up of the bride and groom all teary-eyed and medium shot of the intoxicated best man giving an incomprehensible speech (can you tell I've edited a lot of wedding videos?). Your friend was in charge of *B-roll*, a wide shot of the vows, and the guest's confused reactions to the best man's speech. You kept your camera recording and have long takes—sometimes up to five or ten minutes. Your friend, however, used short takes—no longer than fifteen or twenty seconds each. After the event, you import all of the video media into your editing program. Your camera card has twenty shots, but your friend has over a hundred. How should you name these?

I'd recommend something like this: Go through each of your twenty clips. Give them a name relevant to the main event.

EXAMPLE-1-ORIGINAL-MEDIA-NAME

EXAMPLE-2-ORIGINAL-MEDIA-NAME

Notice how I kept the original media name at the end. Advanced editing systems like Premiere and Resolve can easily *reveal* the original media in your computer's folder. But it's nice to have the name of the file right there in front of you in case you need to reference it. Another method might be to number the media in chronological order. Most cameras already do this, so all you'd have to do is number it 1 through whatever, then type the clip description, then leave the original name.

Now for your friend's clips, I'd suggest something like this:

`001-EVENT-ORIGINAL-MEDIA-NAME`

`002-ORIGINAL-MEDIA-NAME`

`003-ORIGINAL-MEDIA-NAME`

`004-EVENT-ORIGINAL-MEDIA-NAME`

Here, I numbered the media chronologically, but only *named* the media where the setting or event changed. Sitting around naming files all day isn't a great use of your time unless you are shooting a movie or short film or need to meticulously track every moment of your video. For most projects, event-based labeling works fine. I encourage you to experiment and find what works best for you. It could change from day to day, project to project. What's important is once you start a naming convention, stick with it for the remainder of that project.

Cameras and file names: Some cameras -- especially the higher-end cameras -- require the files on the storage device to follow a name convention. If you need to put your videos files back into the camera, then you should <u>not</u> change the file names. Also, don't change the names if you are part of a specific workflow with other people who also require the original final names. In those cases, change the name of the files only in your editing program.

Sequences

Sequences contain the timelines for your video projects. You can make as many sequences as you need within a given project. For complex projects—like versions or drafts of the same video content—you will be using sequences a lot to separate your different edits.

I also recommend a fairly consistent naming convention for your sequences. I'll explain more about how to organize your sequences later in this chapter.

THE MOST COMMON TIMELINE TOOLS

Playhead

The playhead marks where you are working or viewing in a timeline (sequence). You can use the playhead to apply the actions of your tools without needing the cursor to be in the same place. The playhead can jump to wherever you click. Say, for example, you were working at the end of your timeline, but wanted to see something that you did in the beginning. You would just click somewhere near the beginning and your playhead will jump there. Always be aware of your playhead's position. If you're not paying attention, you might apply effects or edits to the playhead instead of where you want it to go.

Cut/Blade/Slice/Razor

The cut or blade tool (and all its other names) slices a clip into two sections on the timeline. You can divide a clip into as many sections or slices as you want. You can even cut down to isolate a single frame if needed. You will be constantly using this tool, so find the cut, blade, slice, or razor tool in your editor of choice. Read the instructions and learn how to use it since there may be more than just a simple slice feature.

Arrow

The arrow tool is how you will select slices/clips and media on the timeline. It's easy to forget to toggle switch to the arrow tool after using something else, like the blade tool. So get in the habit of knowing which tool you're using. Your arrow tool will also have your extra or right-click features. In Premiere or Resolve, if you right-click on a piece of media in the timeline, a box listing many extra options will appear. You can ignore these options for now but they will be useful later as your editing skills grow.

Track

The track tool is another selection tool. You will be using it to select all clips after you place the playhead. You can use the track tool to select all clips on all tracks after the playhead, or select all clips on one particular track. At first, you won't have much need for the track tool; the arrow will get the job done. However, once your timeline gets longer with dozens or hundreds of cuts, you'll love the track tool. What are tracks? I'll explain in the next section.

Q

Zoom

This is the Inspector Gadget tool. Actually that's not true at all. It's called the **zoom** tool and it helps you expand or shrink your timeline. Once your timeline is longer than twenty or thirty seconds, you will need to use the zoom tool. Normally you select the zoom tool, then click to expand the timeline. To zoom out, you would press ALT on your Windows keyboard or Option for Mac, then click. However, the process is different for each program and operating system. If you can't get the zoom tool to work, find the buttons to zoom in and out on your editing software's timeline.

Other editing tools

If you're brand new to editing, I suggest using only the above tools for your first projects. After you become more experienced, you will start wishing you had an easier way to manipulate media and clips. When you get to that point, take a look at these tools:

- Ripple Edit

- Rolling Edit

- Slide

- Hand

Tracks

Each timeline has two *track* sections: video (top) and audio (bottom). Both sections can have multiple tracks and can be layered. Simple videos often use only one or two tracks for each. Complex videos can use dozens.

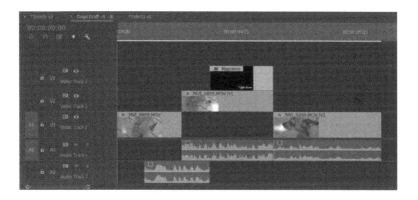

You might ask yourself: "Why do I need layers of video tracks when I can see only one video clip at a time?" The short answer is that layering video helps you organize, time and apply transitions and other effects to your clips.

The goal is to use as few tracks as possible while keeping them organized. I like to put all of my titles above track 3 and all my music on the lowest track available in the audio track section.

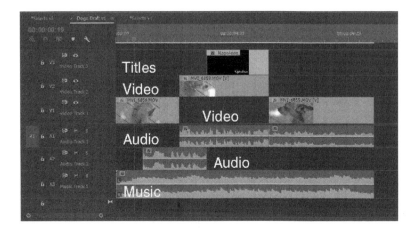

In the advanced editing programs like Premiere and Resolve, you can rename the tracks to match the clips. For example: in the above image, I called track 3 in the video section "TITLES" and track 3 in the audio "MUSIC." This is a more advanced step in organization, so don't worry about it unless it helps you stay organized.

You can click and drag media to any of the tracks within the timeline as you edit. In the video section, the highest track is the track that plays in the program monitor.

LAYERS HELP YOU ORGANIZE YOUR TIMELINE

Layering

Layering is the process of placing media and clips on different tracks in the timeline. As mentioned above: layer order is important for the video part of the timeline. Layer Order is *not* as important in the audio portion. However, organization is important for both.

Adjust the volume to keep your sanity

Adjusting the volume of your individual audio media or the entire track is an intermediate level technique. However, messy audio bothers me, so it might bother you too. Some of your clips will be too loud while others are too quiet. It's possible you will want to mute some audio parts entirely. Here are some ways to quickly adjust your audio.

By clip: You can adjust the audio *level* of an individual audio clip. It can be done by altering either the audio accompanying the video or audio stream alone. Usually you can right-click on the audio clip and a box will appear with options. Look for the words "Gain" or "Levels" or "Volume" in the box. You can also click the clip (a normal left-click) and go to the Audio Effects panel. Whichever editor you're using, search online for "how to adjust audio."

By sequence/timeline: Your editing program could have the ability to change the volume on the track itself rather than the individual audio clips. In Premiere, you expand the audio track by clicking on its lower border and dragging it down. You will see little diamond shapes called *keyframes*.

Keyframes are points you set to change values for media or effects. In the case of keyframes on the audio timeline, you would set a keyframe to raise or lower volume. Keyframes are an advanced topic, but using them on the audio track is the easiest way to learn.

USE TRANSITIONS TO IMPROVE PACING AND PLACEMENT

A transition the change from one clip to another. Do you remember seeing any of the old Batman TV series? The bat logo would zoom in and out between two shots. That is an example of a wacky transition. A more subtle transition is a dissolve, where one clip fades to another. Or a fade-to-black, when one clip fades to... black....

Transitions help you organize your sections and allow you to move from one clip to another with a certain style. I'll better explain the use of transitions when I discuss style.

Dissolve

A dissolve is when a clip disappears as the next clip appears. This is sometimes called a fade, but I refer to a fade when the clip disappears to black or white or to any media other than another video clip. Dissolves are the most basic and most used transition because they are easy on the eyes and brain of the viewer. You can use a dissolve between any two clips and the effect will be smooth.

Push

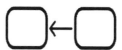

Push is one of my favorite and most-used transitions. It's also one of my favorite Matchbox Twenty songs. A push transition pushes one clip out of frame of the video player or monitor while another clip pushes right in next to it. Think of one clip pushing another clip out of the way. I like it because it's an energetic transition and many times has helped get me out of difficult situations, like when the audio or video don't match but must appear in a specific order.

Flash

Flash transitions are popular and used with just about every style of commercial video. Imagine a person aiming a spotlight into the camera lens, temporarily blinding the viewer. Then the bright light disappears and the viewer is presented with a new image. That is the flash transition effect.

Applying a transition

You have two transition setups: side-by-side or layered clips.

The first method, side-by-side, applies the transition to both clips. This is most apparent with a push transition. As clip A slides to the left, clip B slides right after it. In the second method, the transition is applied to clip B only. So, clip B slides over clip A. Some transitions, like the flash, look slightly different. Another transition, like the dissolve, doesn't look any different.

ENHANCE YOUR VIDEOS WITH TITLES AND OVERLAYS

Titles are text on your timeline. *Overlays* are graphics, effects, or other videos layered on your timeline.

Most editing programs use a separate panel for creating and editing titles. Each program is slightly different, but the concept is basically the same. You create a title clip that goes onto the timeline—the same way a normal video clip goes onto the timeline. You then click onto the title clip and a separate panel will open up for you to edit the text.

When I write overlays, I'm referring mostly to still images or graphics that are layered on the top of your video. These could be fancy titles that have a lot of illustrations or even a tiny video that animates something in and out of the frame. For now, don't waste too much time working with overlays. Work with overlays after you are comfortable with basic editing and clip transitions.

For the more advanced editors, there are two concepts you will need to know when experimenting with titles and overlays:

Opacity: Opacity denotes the transparency of a video or image and is usually measured as a continuum from 0 (invisible) to 100 (completely visible).

Blend mode: Blend mode describes how the image is filtered over the bottom clip. Think of the blend mode as a stained glass window. The light from behind the stained glass can still be seen, but so can the images on the glass itself. They are blended. There are many types of blends, but find out if your software supports blending. If yes, find which different blend *modes* are available.

SAVE YOUR WORK WITH SEQUENCES AND VERSION CONTROL

A *sequence* is a timeline with all of your edits. You can label sequences whatever you like. "Video 1" for example. However, as with folder and file names, I suggest you create a standard with sequence names. Here's an example:

```
Electronics Lesson 5 - Diodes - version 1
```

If that's too long, try something like...

```
lesson5_v1
```

...then keep that sequence under a bin called "Electronics Lessons." The sequence doesn't have to exactly match the title of the video, but if you're editing dozens or hundreds of videos each with its own versions, you'll want a meaningful standard to help you easily distinguish the sequences.

Version control is how you label different drafts of the same video or project. Example:

```
lesson_05_v1
lesson_05_v1-2
lesson_05_v2
```

I create new versions for even the most minor changes. Let's say I open my "Version 1" sequence and I notice I have misspelled a word (or maybe several words in my case). I'll copy "Version 1", then re-title the copy to "Version 2". Then I'll correct my error. Some of my clients can get very picky about details, so every change is important for me to log. Now, that's not to say I make a new version for every individual change. If I receive a note from a client that reads "Fix a spelling error, take out this clip, add this clip," then I'll make all of those changes and just title it "Version 2".

Get to know your media

A major part of editing is simply reviewing your media. Ideally, you want to know all of your audio and video inside and out. If you know your media well, you can draw connections and perform a lot of editing beforehand in your mind. This will make the actual process of cutting up and assembling the clips much more fun.

If you're working for someone else, you may receive a lot of written notes with instructions. Read these notes and connect them to any media they reference. Directors and producers might want to try something different or ask you to change something. If you know the media well, you can give them answers immediately whether or not something is possible.

Use *Markers* to take notes

Organizing and naming your media properly is a great start. After that you'll want to take notes on each individual clip. Some people keep separate text documents for notes. For instance, if you have a clip that is one minute long and the part you want to use is thirty seconds into the clip, you'll write a note like this:

00:30 – Something cool happens.

The advantages of having a separate text document for notes are that you can share them easily with other team members and format notes however you like. The only disadvantage is that it's annoying to be constantly looking back and forth between the notes document and your editing software.

Premiere, Resolve and Final Cut all use something called *markers* to help you write important moments directly onto a clip or sequence. Once you set a marker, you can leave it blank or fill it in with as many details as you need. I recommend using markers or your software's equivalent. Markers will help in organizing important events. Also Markers can be used to help you remember issues like syncing sound or the use of multiple cameras. If you're new to editing, you won't be doing those last two things. However, the practice of using markers will make organizing your complex projects much easier.

Editors should be on set

If you know you will be the editor of an upcoming video recording, I recommend you visit the recording set and take notes. If you can get the *timecode* off of the camera or look at your watch to keep track of the time or how long into a recording when important moments occur, this will help you later in your editing. Trust me, this is not a waste of your time. In addition, it'll make you seem like you're a pro to the rest of the film crew. And you might even get a free lunch.

Organize your media with *Selects*

Now that you are organized, you can finally begin to review and edit. Building your **selects** sequence is the first step to a draft of your video project.

Selects include all of the media you might need and exclude the media you don't need. I wrote 'might need' because sometimes you don't always know exactly which clips will end up in the final video. In my experience, some of the video media which I was one hundred percent sure I needed ended up getting cut. And sometimes the media I thought was junk I ended up using. Life's funny that way.

I'll use this as a reminder to check out the videos at...

videoeditinghandbook.com/videos-e2

This is one of those sections where you'll have to see it to believe it.

How to actually edit your media

This section is for those of you who are completely lost or so new to editing that you just want someone to show you how all this comes together. I tried to guide using prose in the previous editions, but this is one of those processes where you have to see it with your own eyeballs in real time. So be sure to visit videoeditinghandbook.com/videos-e2 and watch the demonstration.

STORY

This question gets philosophical in cinema and art books. But I'm going to skip all of that and assume you have some sense of what "story" means. What I would recommend instead is you keep your sense of story flexible. *Lawrence of Arabia* is a story, but so is a 15 second clip of a child blowing out her birthday candles. The famous story-in-three-sentence goes something like…

Baby shoes. For Sale. Never worn.

And note these aren't even complete sentences, yet if you think about for just a moment, more meaning emerges. Search the internet for "micro-stories" or similar and you'll find some clever authors. Thumb through a book of iconic artwork and notice the stories told in a single frame. Heck, just look at the icons and emojis on your computer and you'll find micro stories.

The point is to be constantly looking for the story. Your editing should not only convey the big story, but all of the little stories that make up the big story.

Editing a Story

Think of editing like writing a story. What does this feel like?

Today. One day only. Best deals.

I led you a bit, but it feels like an advertisement, right? How might a video advertisement accompanying this look? (Check out the video link at the beginning of the book to see.) Spoiler: the video is practically a copy of the text except as frames instead of a sentence on a page. Not very creative, right? But it shows just how blurred the distinction between video and story becomes. Replace those words with images for any generic product sale and you have the same impression.

The shots, like the phrases, are about the same length, with each piece conveying about the same amount of information with the same weight or importance. You can get away with writing and editing like that when you're making an ad. Sometimes you can get away with making movies like this, but usually for certain moments. What about this line?

She looks. Nothing. Did she hear something? At once, a face appears.

How would you convey this in a movie? Watch the demo at the website to find out!

In both examples, the pieces composing the moment vary in length and content. The information in each is not quite equal. Some moments have more importance than others.

If thinking about story is hard for you at first -- it's difficult for me all the time -- maybe set a timer for every twenty minutes or so. When that timer chimes, stop editing and ask yourself: what's the story so far? It's OK to ponder this for a long time. After all this *is* the job. It's not clicking and adding effects.

EDITING DECISIONS

Editing a video might at first seem daunting, especially if it is a long project or you're not confident in the quality of the media you have to edit. The trick to editing with confidence is, in the beginning, to *ignore the details*. Every long or complex edit is built on only a few foundational decisions.

Start with your *Instincts*

First of all, I won't be offended if you skip any part of this book. Diving into your project by throwing stuff on a timeline without the slightest idea of what you are doing is not a bad strategy. Just be aware that you are doing that strategy *on purpose* and it may take longer if you don't have an end goal in mind.

The Four Editing Decisions

Ultimately, you have only four decisions when you're editing:

1. Will the clips go side-by-side?

2. Will the clips be layered?

3. How will the clips be timed?

4. Do you really want to use the clip at all?

These decisions might seem obvious, but articulating them to yourself during stressful times will help you and your clients make decisions quickly. No amazing special effects or cheesy starwipe transitions or titles will help you escape these foundational decisions. Don't know what a starwipe transition is? You're better off that way...

Here are some basic questions to ask yourself when considering when and where a clip should be placed:

- Where am I in editing this video? Beginning? Middle? End?

- What other clips will come before or after this clip?

- Have we seen this clip before or something similar?

- What information does this clip contain? What does it NOT have that I might need?

- Is there anything that makes this clip unusable? Product logo? Equipment? Weirdness?

- Do I need more coffee?

As I mentioned in the Story section, think of each video and audio clip like you would a sentence. Which sentence do you need to set up the story and which sentence should come after that? And finally which sentence will close the story? There are many cinematic theories and marketing ideas to help you decide how to edit. I recommend you study cinematic and marketing ideas after you start to develop your own personal style. Some of the most important ideas I've included in this book. However, at this stage of your study I think it is more important to rely on your own ideas and artistic instincts. An excellent way to measure your results is to watch your audience reactions. By audience I mean your friends, family, and colleagues.

Decision 1: *Side-by-side*

Side-by-side is positioning one clip after another on your timeline. The two clips can be on the same or different tracks, but they cannot overlap. This is the best process for beginners as it is easy to understand the relationship between your clips. Please note that side-by-side is a good format for a music video or vlog.

Decision 2: Layering

Layering is just like it sounds: one piece of audio or video placed on top of another, like a cake. Clip A will be on Track 1, while Clip B will be on Track 2. You can position them over each other however you like. Layering becomes more useful with scenes for a short film (especially dialog) also layering is used often in news videos. On Track 1 you have someone being interviewed. On Track 2 you have B-roll (extra videos) that appear off and on.

Decision 3: Timing

Once you know clips can be only side-by-side or layered, the only other decision you will have to make is the timing of the clips. Timing determines when a clip begins and ends, or when another event happens such as a music cue timed to a character's reaction.

Decision 4: Omission

I once heard Quentin Tarantino say that after he writes a scene, he takes out the last line. If the scene still makes sense, he'll take out the next last line. He keeps doing that until he reaches a line he cannot take out. I apply the same strategy to my own editing when I can.

When a section of your video doesn't seem to be working and you've tried many other versions, try removing the clips/audio before and after the troublesome part. You may have to remove the spot entirely. Watch your new version and ask yourself what is lost or gained by removing this section.

MY GO-TO TRICKS

For many of you, this is the chapter you were waiting for and will refer to most often. Like many skills, video editing uses only a handful of concepts heavily salted with details. Here's a list of basic editing tricks I use routinely. As you develop your own editing style I suggest making a list of your own.

KEYBOARD SHORTCUTS

Keyboard shortcuts allow you to edit without using the mouse. Premiere, Final Cut, Resolve, and most other programs use shortcuts and can be used without any special setup. I began my editing career by using default keys and gradually added my own customized keys as the need arose. For big, repetitive projects, I make temporary shortcuts depending on which tool or process I am using. Keyboard shortcuts, used correctly, save time.

However, there's a tendency in the video community to glorify keyboard virtuosity. Don't get too caught up in all the finger tricks. Personally, I find value in being forced to do things slowly. In some ways, I miss the days when editing required forethought, imagination and reflection. At any rate, these are the shortcuts that you might find most immediately helpful:

- **A** selects the Track Select Forward tool.

- **V** selects the Arrow tool.

- **C** selects the Razor tool.

- **Ctrl K** Makes a cut. Some people just use K or /

- **** Toggles the timeline to view completely or zoom in.

- **D** selects a clip.

- **X** selects an entire clip with in and out points.

- **'** removes the selected clip, saves it to the clipboard and closes the empty space.

- **Ctrl Shift V** pastes a copied/cut clip and moves the rest of the clips after it.

Repetition builds your theme

Repeating a video clip or some variation of a clip is an easy, effective way of giving your project a theme. Movies use repeating segments for recurring flashbacks, twist endings or subtle things the characters are thinking about. Repetition works for non-fiction works as well. If I'm doing an event recap video for a client, I'll often take clips from the beginning and use them at the end to tie things together. Sometimes I will add slow-motion or an extra beginning or ending to the clip. Repetition helps to emphasize the theme of the video.

Match or *oppose* movements

Think of a sports montage—soccer or surfing for example. Naturally, you'll be dealing with video that has lots of movement. One way to approach action-heavy content is to notice the direction of movement on the screen. Different actions on the screen that are moving in the same direction need to be merged together smoothly.

Paradoxically, when there are two video clips with very similar setups or actions, cutting between the two can be startling.

The same concept applies to actions moving in opposite directions. If you want to break from the flow of the first action, use a clip with action going the opposite. This gives a sense of an impending collision or a battle between the two sides, heightening the dramatic effect. Boom!

Double up

This is a great option when you don't have enough video of a certain moment. When I edited sports trailers or recaps, I used this trick a lot.

Imagine you are editing a baseball game. The batter swings and the swing happens to change the game. That's an important moment, but it's short. If you need more time with that moment, cut it and repeat it. Repeat it three times if you need. Make the second or third time slow motion, or black and white. The reverse of those steps works too, especially if you're building up to something.

In a nutshell:

- Repeat clips. Keep them exactly the same or change them.

- Build up to or emphasize the moment

- Give yourself more time with a moment

Un-match

This is more of a storytelling technique, but when used intentionally, the Un-match can act like a sharp turn.

Let's start with an image of a delicate flower pot. Then a big explosion. The two images have nothing in common, but they can sort of tell a story -- if even a twisted one. Now imagine a woman talking on the phone. Then almost the exact same image of the same woman in the same position holding an apple. The images look very similar, but don't really tell much of a story. This demonstrates how much the mind adds to the images.

Use the un-match when you want a striking feeling from the viewer.

Use *Natural hits* as transitions

A ***natural hit*** is something jarring or implying contact within the video itself: a baseball player's crack of the bat, two players high fiving, or a drop of water falling. Even a blink can be a hit. Generally in editing video, and especially for stealth editing, you need to cut onto the hit immediately or sometimes a few frames before. Try the clips in different ways to see what works the best.

Recently I was editing a project in which a guy deliberately crushes a TV with his knee. My first attempt was to cut on the knee impact. I followed with a close up but it didn't look right. So I moved the cut forward a frame, then another, and then another until finally I had cut a full second after the impact.

You can also use some impacts as transitions. When I used to record music concerts, I'd always get a shot of the strobe lights above or another stage light that was above the band. When the lights flashed, I could *cut onto the flash* and use it the same as I would a dip-to-white or flash transition.

Be aware of the hit moments in your video. If you focus on these hits, your video will have an energetic vibe. For videos of rock bands you edit with that purpose in mind.

Use the *L Cut* to layer

Ahhh the classic L cut. You'll be using this A LOT. I've already written about it many times. Here's what an L cut looks like on a timeline.

You don't always want your cuts to match the changes in audio. At least not for more than three or four in a row. Generally, you want to stagger the audio and video changes. This technique works well for documentary or news-type pieces, when your ambient sounds (background noises, cars, wind, crowds) change dramatically from cut to cut. Staggering the transitions between video and audio gives your video a seamless flow.

I also recommend playing with the length of the L cut. You can achieve some interesting results by exaggerating the delay between a new video clip and when its accompanying audio appears.

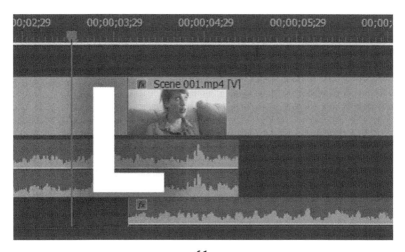

Lastly, let's say you have ten L cuts in a row. When you really want to make an impression, use a straight cut. That will emphasize the moment without any extra cue or effect.

Create *Patterns* then *Break* them

The *pattern-break* cut is used when a clip repeats, then the repetition is interrupted or broken. Patterns can be found within the video. Think of those obnoxious prank videos where the prankster scares people. In those videos the editor shows a montage of victims approaching the same spot. Then, with the final victim, there is no cut. The prankster jumps out and scares the victim. You can also use impact editing to achieve a similar effect. For example: you could edit three clips at one second each and then hold onto another clip for ten seconds.

The scope of the pattern-break technique can be expanded. There may be three 5-second scenes of people doing the same thing. Then in the fourth 5-second scene, it's cut differently. Even if the fourth person does the same thing, the unique cut will break it from the pattern and signal to the viewer that something new is about to happen.

Battle your clips

The filmmaker D.W. Griffith was credited by many cinematographers with being the first to master the technique of cross cutting. **Cross cutting** is cutting between two different clips as the scene is happening. Think of a race-car scene where the two cars are neck and neck. First the focus is one car then quickly moves to the other and then back again to the first, back to the second and so on.

The above stills are from a Machinima video game project I edited. In the scene, cameras 1 and 2 are focused from each character's perspective. Camera 3 is focused on the virtual perspective (or "third-person" perspective) which includes both characters.

Editors of motion pictures use cross-cutting as they build increasing tension towards the climactic ending. Think of *The Dark Knight* when Batman is in the building with the Joker while the civilians and prisoners are stranded on the ferries. You can use it too with just about any format. The exceptions are tutorials or any video with a step-by-step format. If you ever find yourself struggling to decide "which clip should go first," think about the cross-cutting option.

Push and Pushback

One of my favorite transitions is the *push* transition, where Clip B pushes Clip A off the screen. But if Clip A pushes Clip B back off the screen, immediately the viewer senses a relationship between Clips A and B. This somewhat extends the above trick of *Battling clips*. Pushing clips back and forth is great for comparisons, debates, energy, and humor.

Alignment can replace action

The *place* where action happens in your video can be just as important as the *direction* from which it happens. When you have little or no action in your video, the alignment or place where the action happens becomes even more important. It's easy to think of the great cinematic masterworks for lessons in alignment, but I like referring to contemporary commercials as well. I'll refer to the Esa-Pekka video by Apple for this. Not much happens in each frame, so instead, the order of the video clips and their designs generate the excitement. The point of focus, your eye, moves from section to section within the screen.

With phone screens delivering much of the video content, alignment and placement are more relevant than ever. As you compose your cuts, think about which screens, mobile or desktop, your video project is most likely to be viewed.

Alternate speed

You can alternate direction and design, but you can also order clips based on the rate of action. I call this the **slow-fast-slow***(or fast-slow-fast)*. Let's imagine we are processing some surfer footage. We have raw GoPro video that was shot from the camera on the surfer's helmet. It's turbulent footage, bro, with the waves and water splashing everywhere. Whoa, dude. We also have some video shot by the surfer's buddy on the beach. The buddy's clips seem slow when compared to the surfer's GoPro video. Depending on your goal, you can alternate between these two positions for a dramatic change.

As an alternative, we can adjust the actual video speed—or "fast-forward" through the video. For instance, the wide surfer clip is forty-five seconds long, but our time budget is for only eight seconds. We will start with the first two seconds of normal-speed video and cut it. We move to the last two seconds and cut that part. Finally we increase the speed of the middle section by a factor of 500 to 1,000 percent.

Now we have a slow-fast-slow action using only one piece of video. This technique works great for sports and action montages but can be applied as a special effect in other types of video. It's also helpful for when you don't have much video to work with.

Punch in for single-shot variety

I use the punch-in technique for most of my single camera interviews. The audience quickly becomes bored if someone is talking for thirty seconds without a change in camera angle. To add some energy to the video, I'll scale up a cut of the speaker. If the size of the video is at 100 percent of the frame, I'll scale to about 110 or 120 percent.

I can use the punch in for almost any video clip, but the technique is especially useful when I don't have a second close-up camera, or I am limited in the amount of video.

Crop like a farmer

Sometimes part of the frame ruins the rest of the clip. It's not bad to crop or scale your video to remove something. I've found you can get away with about a 30% increase in scale and most viewers won't notice.

For awkward shapes, like vertical cell phone video, the best way to fill the empty space is to:

Scale the same video behind the awkwardly-shaped video until this background video fills the screen.

Then blur it, make it a little darker, and viola. You've filled the screen with relevant imagery.

Check out the *Crop* video on the website to see the demo.

If you have text or titles to use, now might be a good opportunity. Say you interviewed someone and something weird happened behind the interviewee, slightly off to the side. You can crop out the weird activity, then add a list of talking points. Now you've removed the undesirable content and added more information to your moment.

Watch the eyes

When I edit movies or short films, I watch the actor's eye movement. I cue off the actor's eye movements to help me decide where to cut the scene. It's one of my favorite cues. I'm careful about cutting just before or after the actor blinks or shifts his eyes during close ups. Sometimes a focus on eye movement will allow the viewer to see the character's reaction. In a shot when the actor looks from one direction to another, that is an excellent opportunity to cut, as long as the clip following is relevant to the direction which the actor is looking.

Eye movement for scene cuts is useful in videos where a person is the main subject—interviews, modeling, etc. Cutting on a blink can be awkward and just plain weird.

Don't cut on a face like this. In fact, never trust a face like this:

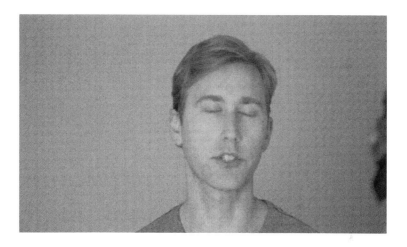

Add a face

Don't have a face to edit? Try to find one, if your content allows. A human face in almost any aspect of content draws more attention than other objects. If you want to quickly grab or sustain attention, include someone's face in your content. There's a reason all those gamers add a little video box of themselves in the corner: it's more interesting to viewers than the gameplay alone.

Maybe you didn't record the speaker on video. Maybe you have only a voice recording. Can you get a nice photograph of the speaker? Even a photograph will help. Say you're giving a lecture on the Second Viennese School, why not throw in a couple of old photos? And the face phenomenon applies to content supporting your video as well, such as thumbnails. Whenever you have video with clear shots of peoples' faces, especially when they exhibit intense emotions, give those shots priority.

Things are people too

In the commentary for his movie *Secret Honor*, Robert Altman said he had to use inanimate objects (such as a portrait, a lamp, and a gun) as characters. There's only one human in the entire feature-length film, the actor Philip Baker Hall. To keep us all from getting bored while watching, Altman uses close ups of and pans to interesting objects around the room. If you have nice close ups of objects, you can achieve a similar effect. Sometimes how or when such an object is shown has a stunning effect.

Notice texture and density

A consequence of endless video and imagery in modern life is losing visual sensitivity. Filmmakers used to be conscientious about the amount of visual information in a shot. For example: a shot of a forest with hundreds of skinny trees might be considered *dense*. Whereas a shot of a hill covered in snow below a grey sky would be considered *sparse*. Filmmakers didn't use these terms officially, but in reading old books about or interviews by filmmakers, I noticed how often they made these considerations. Not too many producers give me notes about density these days, unless a problem occurs for whatever reason. But I still believe, subconsciously, viewers can be affected by these qualities. An editor can still control density for a desired effect.

Swap audio and video for maximum information delivery

Once you learn how to *unlink* the video from the audio and layer clips on top of each other, you can start swapping the video from one clip and audio of another. This is especially useful for sizzle reels, promotional videos, and trailers. Swapping audio and video will help layer the information delivered in the video. Movie trailers do this all the time. They'll have a character's dialog from one scene running while the video from another scene plays over the audio. Swapping audio and video is one of the best ways to convey a lot of information in a short amount of time. This method will help you use the best moments from each piece of unedited video.

Mix and match audio for efficiency

Similar to swapping audio and video, mixing and matching audio can save *runtime*. This is especially true for testimonial-type videos. Let's say there is a recorded event and an important attendee is interviewed. The attendee rambles for several minutes—because champagne was plentiful—but the meaningful audio the editor wants to keep is only a few seconds long. The way I would edit this clip is to play the B-roll over the attendee's audio, then I would chop up the audio so the viewer hears the important part.

Unfortunately, this method doesn't always work. Chopping up what people say and making it sound natural is not easy. Sometimes no matter what I try there is just no way the clip will sound natural.

Stock footage. No shame. Mostly...

We edit in a Golden Age of stock video (usually called stock footage, but maybe we should retire the celluloid words if we're also retiring film). Dozens, maybe even hundreds, of websites offer high-quality video for you to use in your projects. The first point you should understand regarding stock video is licensing. The usage rules have simplified over the years, but you should still take an extra minute to read exactly what you're buying when you're purchasing stock. Hint: if a clip costs $50 for one licensing option and $150 for another licensing option, you can be sure the cheaper option has limitations. For example: that $50 option might allow you to use the video as long as you are *not* selling your final video. Maybe you're making a Public Service Announcement, in which case, that cheap license will work. But if you want to sell your instructional videos on your website, then you'll have to buy the $150 *commercial* license. Not all commercial licenses are the same either. Each seller has a different description of "commercial".

Stock video used to be the laughing stock (get it?) of the post-production world. The videos were typically corny or awkward and didn't work under *any* context. Now the problem is usually the other way around. Stock video tends to be much nicer than what most of us are editing. We can all be grateful, but there's just one problem: it's still stock video. No matter how nice the production quality or how well you cut several, matching stock videos together, it will still feel as generic as a Barbi doll. No one will hate your video, but no one will remember it either. Better to have poor quality but be funny and original than slick and soulless.

Sometimes stock video is unavoidable. Sometimes it's even a good fit. You'll have to be the judge. If you do go with some stock video, here are a few tricks to blend stock video with your own:

Match quality: Say you have video of someone shot under a 3K light and the shadows are a little harsh. Cutting to stock video with a 5K light look and soft shadows might seem out of place. That stock video might look very nice, but consistency in quality is more important than the occasional high-quality shot. If anything, those high-quality inserts will only draw attention to your overall lower production value. Instead, look for clps that match what you already use.

Match look: Most likely your stock videos will have different color palettes or "looks" than your videos. Use a color grading tool (such as Lumetri in Premiere, or the Color panel in Resolve) to match the stock video with your overall look. Often you can apply a look to your entire timeline and that will be sufficient for a draft or quick-turnaround project. But color grading -- also known as *color correction* -- is beyond the scope of this book and is an art worthy of its own book.

Think different: While stock video is better than it was, it should still be considered the last option on your list. So you found an amazing stock clip on page 1 of this website? Great! So did the other 200 editors who were also looking for stock video. Instead, dig around, find clips that are less popular, find clips that could play well together or could be manipulated somehow to elevate beyond just filler video.

Color Grading and Correcting

The process of changing the color and tones of a video is called *color correcting* or *color grading*. Every movie, television show, and most other professional productions have been extensively color graded. So keep that in mind when comparing your own work to a professional video. Professional producers spend thousands of dollars on the color correcting process and for an amateur editor the color corrected look is difficult to achieve, especially if you're using more affordable programs.

Color grading is *not usually* part of the editing task. However at times editors are expected to provide color correction as part of the service. It's not an easy task but there are a few things an independent editor can do to control the quality of the color and tones. Color correcting should be the *last step* in the editing process; an editor must be absolutely sure no more editing changes will be needed before continuing to the color grading process.

Search online for tutorials addressing these concepts:

- Crushing the blacks and whites (or the S curve effect)
- White balance

Keep it snappy

Ever had to watch one of those HR videos made in the 90s about sexual harassment in the workplace? I saw a series which used a long, slow, unnecessary effect of a vault door opening and closing between each section. Maybe in the 90s before people had attention spans of hummingbirds you could get away with that. But these days, just get to the point. Watch any successful YouTube channel and you'll see the videos start right away with an introduction -- sometimes called a "cold open" -- followed by a short bumper or title. I'd say drop the bumper even. This doesn't mean to make short videos. This means include only the best stuff in your video.

Common ways to accomplish this include:

Cut off the moment: whether it's an interview or a snowboarding trick, try to cut as close to the "good stuff" as possible. Try cutting off what is obviously too much, then edit your way backwards, adding a few more moments.

Avoid slow transitions: this includes not only editing transitions like dissolves, but also moment transitions, like a slow pan from a mountain to the subject in the foreground. If you're making a movie or documentary in which you can establish a slower pace, this isn't so bad. But for most commercial and business videos, find a way to get to the next topic faster. In fact, this is where faster editing transitions can help you the most: moving more-naturally from one moment to the next.

L-cut: make liberal use of the L-cut. An L-cut is when the audio of Clip A continues to play even while Clip B appears, or vice versa. This overlap might last for only a few frames, or it can last for several seconds. Try to make your clips "step on each other". You can go too far with this strategy, but beginning edits usually have the opposite problem of not cutting tightly enough.

Reduce redundancy

This falls more under the marketing category, but thinking about the context for your video will help design better content.

The three main requirements an editor will want to know before editing a video for any platform include:

The dimensions of the player windows (i.e., 1920x1080 or 640x640)

Play counts (i.e., 3 seconds or longer) and play limitations (i.e., no longer than 60 seconds)

Information that can be posted around/with the video (i.e., will the video have a text title to help with context? Or a Call to Action button that can be added later?)

Knowing the dimensions of the player windows is important for choosing clips that fit well within that frame. You can also ask yourself "how will my video be seen?" If you expect people to watch on desktop computers or from a projector, you can use smaller fonts and more details. If most people will watch on a phone, you might have to recompose your edits completely.

Requirement 2 determines what an editor will place at the front of the video. With only three seconds to capture a viewer's attention, the most eye-catching images need to be placed in the first part of the clip.

In requirement 3, the information displayed outside the image, is difficult to decide. For example: If the editor knows his video will always have a title above it for the viewer to read, he will not need to repeat that title again within the video. Instead, the editor can add extra information in the video's text.

Redundant information

To summarize: Research the platform you're interested in. Most have a page listing their own conventions and requirements. Don't waste any valuable seconds of video time. When editing, it's better to have too much speed rather than being too slow. The most interesting and fascinating imagery should be at the beginning of the video.

Be a screen real estate agent

Back to design for a moment. An editor must have a good idea where the video will be displayed. The type of device makes your editing decisions even more specific. The main concept you want to learn here is *screen real estate*.

Screen real estate is the setting in which your video will play. A movie theater screen is a different experience from watching a movie on your phone. If you watch *Lawrence of Arabia* on your phone, you're going to miss a lot of things. Vice versa. If you watch a Facebook video ad on the big screen, much of it will spread past your field of vision and will probably give you a seizure.

Adjusting your editing to different screen sizes is not necessarily difficult, it just takes some forethought. Are you editing a short film? That will probably be seen on a desktop monitor, TV, or small theater screen. Editing an ad for the internet? The biggest anyone will probably see it is at the desktop level. The most common will probably be on a mobile device.

So what does this mean? It means if you have text in your video, it needs to be big enough to see. It means if you have an awesome landscape shot, but the person of interest is two hundred feet away, the viewer on a mobile device won't see it. So you'll have to use the medium close-up instead.

Some problems are not as obvious. Let's say you have an eerie musical piece with a lot of low tones, maybe it's for a horror-film trailer. It might sound great on your headphones, but if you're editing this trailer to share on Facebook, people viewing on their phones might not hear that music well. So you better make sure you have visuals which are good enough to carry the interest when the music fails.

Fortunately, with most editing programs, you can change the size of your program window. When I'm editing a short film, I like to stop editing, make the program monitor full screen, step back, and watch the video from a distance. It makes me feel like a painter. When I'm editing for mobile video, I like to make the program monitor very small. Sometimes I'll even export a video, upload it as a private video on YouTube and watch it on my phone. Gives me the full experience.

As you edit, keep in mind your intended screen. It's easy to get caught up in all of the good video clips and forget how people will eventually view it. If it helps, put a sticky note on your monitor with the intended or ideal screen.

Watch out for Copyright and Content ID

Again, this is not usually the editor's problem, but often editors are responsible for catching these issues. Big platforms have content identification (ID) systems. Meaning, if I upload a popular song or clip from a favorite movie, the ID system will catch it and flag my video. Even if you were recording a basketball game and a popular song started playing over the speakers, some content ID systems will still flag your video, especially on YouTube. They are very sophisticated. You ask, what does it mean to be flagged? It depends. Usually I will not be able to monetize the video. Other times, the platform might simply remove my video. If I want either my videos or my channels to have long, profitable lives, I have to avoid getting flagged and I have to avoid copyright infringement. Instead, I use resources I have found to supply my videos with non-copyright music. There is a list of copyright-free music in the Resources section.

Special note about using copyrighted video content: For those of you who intend to edit your own movie review vlog on YouTube: Beware. Using short scenes from movies, shows or even other YouTube videos can get your video flagged. You might benefit from reading YouTube Terms and Services documentation as well as the most recent copyright rules.

For those of you who intend to edit professionally, either as an independent contractor or with a company, you should investigate the Terms and Conditions of *any* of the platforms you want to use. Normally this is the **producer's** job, but at times, for one reason or another, I have had to do it myself. Even if you are making videos just for fun and not making any money off of them, you still need to pay attention to content ID.

Psyche yourself

We're getting into psychology, of which I'm not qualified to coach, so I'll leave you with just a few suggestions... for now.

Don't just sit and edit: From what I've researched and from personal experience, creativity declines with inactivity. Get up and walk or move around every twenty minutes or so. If you're on a roll and feel inspired, keep going until you reach the first slowdown or challenge.

Rest your eyes: The biggest drawback to editing, especially as a career, is the screen time. Keep your eyes healthy by taking breaks, using dark modes, experiment with different monitor settings, and follow the 20-20-20 rule: every twenty minutes, look at something twenty feet away for at least twenty seconds. I've learned the hard way to practice eye fitness. I advise you to take it seriously as well.

The only fonts that will survive

Never underestimate the power of good fonts. The correct choice and placement of fonts is a time consuming but necessary task. Many fonts have the same lifespan of a hashtag and a popular font today may appear dated in a year or two. Nevertheless, I try to make notes listing interesting fonts and where those fonts will work in my videos. The title of this section is an exaggeration, but here is a list of fonts that, in my opinion, are here to stay.

1. Arial Black

2. Bebas Neue

3. Helvetica

4. Impact

5. Open Sans

Good titles, if used properly, will increase the impact of a video.

Arial Black IMPACT
BEBAS NEUE helvetica
open sans

One time I was asked to edit a video to be used by one business to sell a product to another business. The business didn't have all the right raw video I needed to give the intended impression. In order to convey the right information, I had to use some catchy titles and cool fonts. So in this particular case the use of titles replaced the absence of good video clips.

I first wrote this observation about fonts seven years ago. So far, nothing has changed.

STAY ORGANIZED

As the saying goes: Falling in love is easy, staying in love is harder. The same holds true for organization.

Here is an example from my own life:

I was editing a video for a client. He gave me some notes, I made some changes. The client then gave me more notes. I made more changes. Then the client called me to say, "I think I like the version you showed me when you first started. Which one was that?" Then I looked at my one lone timeline sequence and thought, "Oops."

Moral of the story: *make a new sequence for each version of your video*. This is the same message I gave you in the first chapter pertaining to organization. It applies as much during your editing process as it does before you begin the project.

Be careful with new media and updates

As I edit, the client may send me some new video along with new effects and audio. I may be tempted to not spend any time organizing the newly imported items, especially when I'm near the end of a project. However, I'm always thankful later when I take an extra few minutes to organize and label the new media.

Naming each version of the media is as important as naming each version of the sequences. If I am working on more advanced projects with visual effects, I will be changing and tweaking the effects as I edit. Rather than deleting the old versions of effects or replacing them, I always keep the older versions by labeling the updates "version 2" or "v2" for the version with which I am working. Since I never know when I will need to refer to an older version, I save all the data.

MEDIA CACHES CAN EAT UP HARD DRIVE SPACE

Media caches are folders where data is stored that links to a project. Let's assume I need to import a certain type of audio to use with a project. I require the editing software I use to be able to *encode* the audio into a different *file format* so I can begin my editing. The software needs to store this encoded media in a media cache folder in my computer's hard drive. If I am working with a lot of video, especially raw or Ultra HD video, media cache folders will use a lot of space in my computer.

For your own editing, I recommend you determine if your editing software can cache media and where the software stores the media. You can usually *clear the cache* by using one of the program's menu options. If not, you will have to manually delete the files by navigating to the folder and delete the media there.

Usually you'll find the cache options under the *Preferences* of your editing software.

Deleting the cache: I do not recommend that you delete the media cache files unless you're completely familiar with the project and the editing software. It will not be fatal to your project if you accidentally delete the wrong media, but you will have to use your editing software to encode the media again.

CREATE VERSIONS OF YOUR PROJECTS

For really big and complicated projects, I will sometimes create an entirely new version of the project instead of copying the new sequences within the project. The benefits of doing this are:

A new project version helps me to organize the media and sequences.

If, as sometimes happens, one project version becomes corrupted, I still have some other versions of the entire project.

Some projects have so much media and data that a separate project version is the only way I can keep track of the versions. For example: I edited a YouTube video in which the producer used six cameras and video files were huge and cumbersome. In addition, the producers made multiple revisions. Rather than revise the sequences within the project, I made entirely new project files and labeled them "Project v1", "Project v2", and so on.

Every editing system has its idiosyncrasies. Occasionally my project version will become corrupted and fail to boot up. Or if it boots up it won't function properly. The use of multiple project versions minimizes lost time should these things happen. Premiere Pro will automatically save versions, so if the system crashes I can readily find an older saved version. When using any editing software I recommend you periodically save your versions, which allows you to control the naming and timing. If you choose not to use different versions of your project, I recommend you manually make back-ups. It's a great habit to have and you will thank yourself if the worst ever happens.

The only disadvantage when using different versions for a project is when I need to transfer my new edits to an older project version. For example, I am working on my project when I realize the older version is better visually and I have installed a lot of new titles in my most recent version. Normally transferring work from one version to another is a tedious process, however more robust editing applications make the transfers much easier because they offer an import feature. When choosing your editing software you may want to determine how well the software can import older versions of your project from the cache.

EXPORT, DELIVER, STORE

You have finished editing your first video. High fives all around. Now what are the next tasks? First, you will need to format your video into media you can share. This process is called **exporting**. Every video editing software has an export option. Depending on which program you're using, exporting can be called *saving*, **rendering**, *exporting*, or **transcoding**. Normally the exporting option is in the "File" or "Edit" menu of the editing software.

When exporting the entire sequence, the program renders all the processed video into a single file. This file can end with any of the following extensions; .mp4, .mov, .avi, or .3gp (for cell phones). There are many video formats, but for the purposes of this book, the six I will list are the most common for general use. Here's a quick summary of when to use each format:

.mp4

MP4 (also MPEG-4) is a digital multimedia file. You'll hear concepts like **codec** and **file format**, but those are more details than you need at this time. For further reading you can refer to the glossary or search online. It is important to know the .mp4 format is one of the most common video formats you will use when exporting your projects. YouTube prefers the .mp4 format as do Vimeo and many other online video platforms. The .mp4 format can also be played on most operating systems.

At some point in your editing you may need additional file formats. If you are uncertain about what you need, export the project with a high **bit rate** .mp4 file. Most situations can use .mp4.

.mov

MOV is another common format. It is called the container format because it can store files with different file extensions. Unlike the .mp4 file by itself, the .mov file can play only with QuickTime (Apple/Mac) framework. If you're trading videos from Mac to Mac, then you won't have a problem. Most popular video hosting websites also accept .mov files for upload.

Personally, even if I'm working in a Mac-only environment, I still prefer .mp4 because of its flexibility of use for all platforms.

.avi and .wmv

AVI and WMV are called container formats. Both extensions were developed by Microsoft and the .avi format is gradually declining in use. These days, I use .avi for only lossless video. Meaning, no information is lost when the .avi file is created. When I export a project using the motion graphics program After Effects, I will export videos as .avi files. With a Mac system I will export the file using a .mov extension. However, all these systems are changing. An important fact you need to remember is that the file extensions .avi and .wmv are both compatible with Windows systems. Also remember that almost all video hosting sites will accept the .wmv format.

.3gp

Though now less common as a recording format, 3GP format is used primarily for mobile devices. When a video is streamed through the internet using a cell phone's data plan, the video file has a .3gp file extension. One day you may have to export a video with a .3gp file. Or perhaps, you may be given .3gp files as an editing project (I'm sorry if that happens). More commonly, you will upload your video to a hosting service and the service will convert your video into a .3gp format. Again, just like with .avi, I want to make you aware of the existence of this common format, even if you'll rarely use it.

ProRes

ProRes is a video compression format developed by Apple and functions on Mac or QuickTime systems. ProRes files are used when editing with Final Cut Pro or Final Cut X. ProRes allows video media to retain high quality yet doesn't lose speed in the process. It is necessary to have Apple's Final Cut editing program installed on a Mac computer in order to use ProRes. There are some methods to work around this exclusivity but they are beyond the scope of this book. Also, in early 2017, the Premiere developers announced their program will support ProRes on the Windows system. I have read some complaints of Premiere users having limited success exporting ProRes or transferring their project between the Mac and Windows systems. At this time, I'd recommend NOT using ProRes if your computer is a Microsoft Windows machine until the bug is fixed.

To summarize this chapter: Most of the time when exporting files you will export using the .mp4 format.

MY GO-TO EXPORTING TOOLS

Listed below are my go-to exporting tools and resources.

Mpeg StreamClip and compressing

Mpeg StreamClip is a free **compression** program. It can read most video file formats and is great for compressing several videos from one session into another format. What is *compressing?* Compression means either making a video file smaller or better suited for another program to process. Another compression program that I use is Adobe Media Encoder. If you don't have access to Adobe Creative Suite, I recommend StreamClip for your compression requirements.

Simply search online for "wondershare mpeg streamclip" to find a site from which you can download the program to your computer.

Handbrake and encoding

Handbrake is a free video **transcoder** used to convert digital video into another digital format. For instance, it may be necessary to transcode an .avi media file into an .mp4 file, which can then be loaded onto a server which will not process .avi media. **Encoding** is a different process. Encoding is the method used to convert analog media into digital format. Think of turning something *into code*. An example of encoding is transferring a cassette tape to an .mp3 format. Some people mistakenly use these terms, encoding and transcoding, interchangeably to describe the transfer of one digital format to another digital format. Be sure to confirm the difference between the two in case someone asks you to perform either task. In most cases, people mean *transcoding*: transitioning from code to different code.

Handbrake has a "compress video" feature similar to Mpeg StreamClip. I generally use Handbrake to convert DVDs into .mp4 files. If I am doing a video job for a client for which I want to use a motion picture scene downloaded from a DVD I will use Handbrake to convert the DVD format into an .mp4 file.

Handbrake can be easily found online by searching "handbrake".

Adobe Media Encoder

AME is Adobe's proprietary encoding software. Even though it is possible to directly export video from Premiere or After Effects software, I always export video using AME for the following reasons:

AME allows me to queue several projects at the same time. Exporting via Premiere forces me to export a video one at a time.

While AME is exporting files, I can continue editing another project with Premiere

To use AME, I don't have to open up the Premiere application. I can simply drag and drop a video or audio format into the AME encoder. AME is frequently updated because it is linked to the

Adobe Creative Suite. AME has a large list of templates for file formats. For example, if I am uploading a video to the Vimeo website, AME has several Vimeo format options from which to choose.

Mac's Compressor

Final Cut X is packaged with Apple's compressor features. Apple's very original, "think different" name for their compressor software is *Compressor*. This feature compresses and encodes similar to the Adobe Media Encoder or Mpeg Streamclip program. For those editors using iMovie or any non-Adobe, non-Apple editor, Apple's Compressor can be purchased separately from the App store. Editors intending to use Compressor for all their projects, may want to consider buying the complete Final Cut X editing software which includes Compressor.

A *PLATFORM* IS YOUR THEATER

When people talk about video hosting and delivery, the word *platform* comes up a lot. Platform, in a loose definition, just means a particular software or service. Windows is a platform for operating software. Pandora is a platform for listening to music. YouTube is a platform for uploading video. For this book, the most important platforms are video hosting and sharing/delivery services.

YouTube is both a hosting and sharing platform. *Hosting* platforms allow videos to be uploaded. *Delivering* or *sharing* platforms allow videos to be sent to other computers or servers.

I have a server which I can upload and host videos, but my server does not provide any built-in tools to share my videos. Some smaller websites will allow the user to share videos via a YouTube or Vimeo link, but will not permit uploads.

In the beginning, which platform an editor chooses to use as a host is not critical. As the editor's fan or consumer base grows and if he or she begins to experiment with technology, perhaps virtual reality or 360 degree cameras, the editor will need to be more choosy when picking a hosting platform. Also an editor needs to think about specific platform options for sharing: privacy controls, upload speeds, and team sharing.

Deplatforming (the not-so-obvious reasons): Another consideration that comes up a lot these days is de-platforming. That's when a hosting provider kicks you off its platform. People hear about all of the controversial reasons, but many mundane reasons are just as common. A host could go out of business -- VRideo, Vidme, and Vine come to mind; A host could "pivot" towards different content -- Netflix and Amazon used to allow almost anyone to upload to their services at one point; A host could just be stupid -- plenty of colleagues and companies I've worked with got flagged or canceled for reasons beyond understanding.

This could be you…

Here are a few questions an editor should ask when deciding to use a specific platform.

How many editors will be working on this project?

What's the size of the project? (Minutes? Hours? Megabytes? Terabytes?)

How long will the video be posted on the platform? (Forever? Temporarily? Until something in particular happens?)

What's the purpose of the project? (A campaign? A vlog/tutorial? An event? A demonstration?)

Who will be the audience? (Just my team? Friends and family? The entire universe?)

What is my relationship with the platform? Am I at its mercy? Or will it work with me in case I have problems?

I will prioritize this list for each project. For example, if I am working with a team of editors or producers, I will build a video easy to share and to organize. If I am working alone and my objective is to grab as many viewers as possible, I'll have to make a project simple to share and easy to track.

HOSTING VERSUS DELIVERING VERSUS SHARING

These three terms can be used interchangeably, but, ultimately, have different meanings. Hosting means a server or computer holds your videos files, but does not provide any tools for playing or sharing. The term *Sharing* means a service sends a link or embed of your video to another party for them to watch. The term *Delivering* means a service sending the video file itself or a link to that file. Simply put, remember the term sharing equals to link and to play. The term delivering equals file and download.

That's a little confusing, so here's a nice chart to help.

VIDEO DELIVERY OPTIONS

Services for hosting and delivering

The services listed below are satisfactory sites for hosting/delivering but cannot be used for sharing.

DropBox

Dropbox is a general-purpose file sharing service. It's a straightforward and easy-to-use website and great for sending and downloading small or large amounts of video files. However, when video files are hundreds of gigabytes, problems will occur with Dropbox. Downloads will be slow or completely fail at these large sizes. Still with smaller file downloads, sending via DropBox is an easy way to send video along with any other files. I will usually divide larger files by breaking them down into folders. Then, I will send the folders one at a time. DropBox offers a free version of its software however a full access paid subscription is not expensive.

WireDrive

The developers of WireDrive call themselves a media management company. WireDrive is a business-to-business media sharing and delivering service and is more expensive than a consumer-facing service like Dropbox. For the increased cost, the professional user is provided with more features for sharing and organizing videos. If a user is willing to pay the price, WireDrive is the best solution for sharing and delivering videos with your team members clients.

WeTransfer

For a low budget freelance video editor, WeTransfer is a good way to send a draft or final version to a customer. The free version of WeTransfer allows video transfers of 2 gigabytes or less. That's enough for most HD mp4 files under twenty minutes. It's not necessary for the recipient to save the video. WeTransfer will host the video for a few days and then automatically delete it. This feature is useful if I am sending a draft to someone who's not part of my team or my client's team.

Hightail

Hightail is an application which has features like those of DropBox and WireDrive. Hightail is a good solution for small companies or very active freelance editors. This program has the speed and organization of WireDrive and the affordability and user-friendly side of DropBox. It doesn't have as many features as WireDrive, but it is a good choice if you need to send a lot of large files to different people and need to keep track of who got what.

Amazon Drive

Amazon Drive is essentially the same service as DropBox or Google Drive, except less costly for large file storage. Amazon's cheap file storage is the platform's only advantage. The interface is not intuitive because the sharing features are complicated and cumbersome. Besides being able to store a terabyte of files on the cheap, Amazon has some other storage options available. I recommend Amazon but only to editors who have enough ability and patience to learn its idiosyncrasies.

A bit more about sharing

I need to clarify *sharing* a little more. The term sharing also implies immediate playback. When I send out a YouTube link, a viewer can watch the video immediately. When I send out an Amazon Drive or Google Drive link, the viewer has to download the video before viewing it. In a later chapter I will write about sharing on YouTube, Facebook, and other social platforms. The following services offer a blend of sharing and instant-play services as well as hosting and delivery services.

Vimeo

Vimeo is the so-called "artist's" platform. The story is that Vimeo supports a higher-quality encoding than YouTube. Also it is said Vimeo offers a better file-sharing feature than YouTube. Vimeo owns two other platforms, Vimeo OTT andWipster. I find Vimeo most useful when embedded on your personal website or when used in a more private situation. For example, if you're making six videos to teach your employees about internet security, Vimeo is a better option than YouTube. YouTube prefers your videos be as public as possible. Since Vimeo uses a subscription model, they just want you to be happy, so they give you the tools to do what you want.

Wipster.io

Wipster is the best service for fast-turnaround between members of the same creative team. Wipster is a good choice if an editor's work doesn't require the need to send copies to clients outside the organization. For members of a team using Wipster it's easy to upload, organize, and share comments. Each comment is labeled with the name and date of the writer of the comment. Multiple editors are able to indicate to which specific point of the video they are editing. As I mentioned before, Wipster is owned by Vimeo and the two services integrate well.

How to judge other video sharing options

How do you choose which hosting provider for your videos? You have more options available than ever, but you also have more pitfalls than ever. Here are some big considerations before choosing a video host:

Importance of videos: How crucial are videos to your project? If you're an online learning source, then videos might be your main products, thus you *must* ensure your videos play all the time. If you use videos to demonstrate your new smoothie maker, then videos are a nice tool, but you do not require them to make sales. If your videos are important, don't rely on a service like YouTube or Vimeo or Twitter. They can drop your videos or shutdown without notice for any reason. Instead, host your videos yourself with a private host provider such as AWS S3 or DreamHost. You're less likely to get shut down using these hosting providers. But as we've seen recently, even Amazon removes hosting for customers if the internet giant deems it necessary. You might need multiple providers if you feel concerned about losing your video hosting. And note: you don't have to be publishing controversial content to get removed. Someone could send a bogus complaint against you, which might get you suspended until you state your case. In short: the less you pay for hosting, the more likely a host can nix you.

Time: Do you have a lot of time to manage videos? For example: AWS S3 storage is relatively cheap for hosting a lot of videos, but can be a real pain to organize and maintain. On the other hand, Vimeo might help you organize your videos, but is more expensive and has limitations. If you don't have much time or expertise, avoid bare-bones hosting providers like S3. Instead, use a video platform like Vimeo. I prefer Vimeo over YouTube because with Vimeo, you're a paying customer. They'll answer your email. YouTube doesn't have much support for users and they can leave you hanging.

Budget: Do you have a lot of money to spend on video tools? The budget-friendly solution is YouTube, without a doubt. But as mentioned above, for all that free stuff, you take a risk. If your budget is huge, you can go with a service like Vimeo's premium plans or Wipster (now owned by Vimeo). These are excellent tools for sharing videos internally at a company and publicly.

Control: Do you need complete control over your videos? Or can you exchange control for convenience? If you're just publishing commercial videos for your product, you likely don't care how people share or use the video. The more eyes, the better. But if you're a journalist and the integrity of your video and its publication determine your believability, you'll want full control over how the video gets displayed and shared. YouTube is not a great option for controlling your video, but it might be a good option for disseminating it. You might require a private host for full control over your videos, which usually means a paid option.

To summarize, paid options are almost always the way to go if you want control and reliability. YouTube and similar free platforms are mostly for sharing videos, especially if your goal is to reach a wide audience. But these sharing platforms should not be used as your sole video hosting provider.

Retire your video projects with the intention of returning

Once an editor has created a lot of videos, storage becomes a critical problem. Video files seem to grow bigger and bigger over time requiring affordable and reliable storage. Inevitably, you will need to return to a distant project and will benefit from proper, long-term storage.

THE CONUNDRUM OF LONG-TERM STORAGE

Online storage is simply cloud-based storage. Editors can upload their project data to a cloud-storage provider. I mostly use S3 (part of Amazon Web Services, aka AWS) for my cloud storage needs. *For self storage* an editor will keep his project on private hard drives. Below I have listed advantages and disadvantages of both types of storage.

Online Storage Advantages

Redundancy: Online storage providers backup their data on multiple servers. The odds of a cloud-based storage company losing all of an editor's data is statistically small. If an editor's hard drive crashes, is stolen or his house burns down, data stored online is not affected.

Organized: Since all of the data is stored on the provider's server, and as the project develops over a period of time, each change is recorded. Of course an editor can organize files on his own personal hard drive, but with less efficiency.

Online Storage Disadvantages

Slow uploads: Uploading and downloading large video files to the cloud is slow and time consuming; 500 gigabyte files take a lot of time to transfer. And as with anything on the internet, privacy will need to be balanced with convenience.

Offline Storage Advantages

Fast: When it's necessary to move large files with lots of data from computer to computer, using portable hard drives is the most efficient solution.

Control and Privacy: Even though it is more difficult to organize content using several different hard drives, the editor retains full control over privacy and placement of all the data. This is best for sensitive projects. Say you were editing a video featuring a whistleblower's testimony. Sending drafts of that video or saving the raw media online might be a risk you and the producer are not willing to take, even if the service is well-encrypted.

Offline Storage Disadvantages

Expense: At first it may seem like a good idea to buy a 1-terabyte drive for fifty bucks instead of paying one hundred dollars every year to a service provider, but in the long run, I think home storage is more expensive. Here's why: Any serious editor will burn through a 1-terabyte drive like a snowflake in a furnace. An editor can expect to buy a half-dozen drives within the first year of her professional editing career. For safety's sake, hard drives should be checked for corruption every month. The sad fact is that hard drives will sometimes break beyond repair and then all data is lost. Home storage requires each drive be labeled as to its contents. To avoid the frantic search for specific files, there is technology which may be purchased to enable the reading of multiple drives at once. Again, more expense for the editor. All these expenses begin to add up to some serious money or at least more money than the fees charged by the online storage websites.

In the beginning of an editor's career, it is best to use DropBox, YouTube, Vimeo and WeTransfer for storage of data. These platforms provide most storage and transfer requirements and all offer free, less-robust versions of their software. Once an editor becomes more proficient and requires more features than the free versions offer, DropBox premium or Amazon or Google Drive are good choices. In summary, the novice editor is usually better served by using online storage as opposed to self-storage because of cost and safety concerns. As you become a well-paid professional, local or offline storage becomes more useful.

DEVELOP A SYSTEM FOR HANDLING PROBLEMS

It has been my experience that my worst editing problems occur when I am trying to export files. My friend and video technology expert, Tal Levitas, who founded OutPostVFX, suggested to me the following:

If the program crashes when attempting to export, I should try exporting only a small part of the video file. By transferring small portions of the video I may be able to isolate the problem spot that is not allowing the entire video to render. If one section won't transfer I will re-edit the problem section. This technique of isolating problem spots helps me in other phases of the editing process as well.

Check out the video by the same title as this section for more detail. If you need a refresher of the ideas, just consult this list:

If the problem is on the timeline:

Turn off a layer and play the trouble spot. Keep turning off layers one at a time until you can change the problem. Usually the problem comes from a certain clip or multiple clips that don't "layer well" together. Sometimes you can re-create the same edits in a different part of the timeline, then drag them to where you need them.

Try a new project. Copy the trouble spot, open a new project, paste the copy into the new project. If the problem persists, then the problem might be from the video asset itself and not the timeline.

Scrub over the trouble. Sometimes playback causes the problem but not scrubbing. If scrubbing doesn't show the same problem, you can assume exporting the project will not include the problem either.

If the problem is from an individual piece of media:

Re-import. Sometimes it's not the clip that's the problem, it's how the software imported it. You might have to move the media clip out of the computer or harddrive folder, allow the software to realize the clip is missing, then move the clip back into the folder, then re-import. Every piece of software is different, so this might require you to experiment.

Import into a new project. As with timeline problems, sometimes the project file itself (such as a Premiere project file) will just crash on you. A new project will show you whether or not the clip itself has problems, or if your project has problems.

Transcode. Sometimes a media format just doesn't work well with an editing software. Find out which formats work best for your editing suite and transcode the media to that ideal format. Sometimes an entire project requires transcoding if the original media is an unconventional format. But these days, most editing applications support most formats.

Again, check out the video by the same title on the website. I will likely add more and more debugging videos. This is a problem that plagues most editors.

SHARING AND GETTING VIEWS

"How to get more views" is a popular search term. This is not traditionally the job of an editor, but many of you read this book with ambitions to not only create something, but to promote it. And more often than not, video producers at smaller companies are responsible for designing marketing plans to promote the videos. Some of you might already have a built-in audience, such as employees at your company who must watch your videos to learn about a new product or feature. But many of you will be starting from zero and want to build a public audience. Here are some commons practices to get you started:

CREATE GOOD CONTENT

This seems obvious, right? But producers get surprisingly lazy or opportunistic and forget this rule. I've watched millions of dollars in start-up money get poured down the drain because the executives forgot this rule.

How do you create good content? Lots of ways! However, the unavoidable reality for most of us is to start by making bad content. You won't make bad content on purpose, but if you're new, you can't prevent yourself from making a few stinkers. That's ok. We all start this well. Know that you'll get better with each new video.

Don't listen to Apple; don't try to be *different*. Instead, be *interesting*. Different things can be boring. Interesting things, by definition, will never be boring. Michael Crichton said on *Charlie Rose* once that everything he (Crichton) tried to "hit it out of the park", he always failed. But if he wrote what he found interesting, he'd write a great novel. Take note of the things you find interesting. Which books or channels do you constantly refer to? What keeps you up at night? Which images burn into your mind? Then, straight up copy these ideas. Don't worry so much about copyright or "stealing" ideas initially. By the time you're finished with your project, most people won't recognize from where you "stole" it anyway. After more practice, you won't be taking ideas from others as much; you'll have found your voice.

There's a balance with content as well. A good production can sometimes help bad content, but only a little. Whereas good content can greatly help bad production. I call this "charm". Your content needs personality more than it needs great lighting and effects. But charm takes research and experimentation and playfulness. Be prepared to spend a lot of time digging for the ideas to make your content good.

PUBLISH CONSISTENTLY

I'm a bit more ambivalent about this tip. No doubt, if you publish a video each week, you'll likely accumulate more views than if you post every month. But if your quality suffers from the stress of weekly publishing, that can impact the enthusiasm of your audience. If you can manage consistent content, you'll hang onto your audience even with mediocre content. But if you make amazing content, you'll audience will wait as long as it has to.

GET CONSTANT (QUALITY) FEEDBACK

Whether you're building your audience or already have one, this tip applies to everyone. However, quality feedback is also difficult to get. When you're doing something right, you'll know it. You'll see excited comments, shares or purchases pile up. We call this activity *engagement*. Engagement can be defined loosely as: viewers interacting with your content. Comments and sharing are signs of engagement. If a video has lots of views but low engagement, that's a sign that the publisher of the video might be buying views. This isn't always the case, but nevertheless, hosting platforms like YouTube might *throttle* (aka stop recommending) your video if the view count is much higher than the engagement. So long as you're not intentionally trying to buy more views, this is unlikely to happen to you.

Ask your viewers directly for feedback. This might make you feel like you're pandering, but it's not. You probably don't know your audience and this is a good way to find out. Keep a notebook of all your direct feedback. That's how the second edition of this book got created. Several readers commented on Amazon and sent me direct messages. I kept track of all this information and used it to improve. And I'll do it again with the third edition. And forever!

However, keep this quote in mind: "Trust yourself when all men doubt you, yet make allowance for their doubting too." That's from Rudyard Kipling and what that means to me is: listen to others, but also listen to yourself. Just because one person criticizes or praises something about your work doesn't mean you should automatically change anything. It's just one data point of hundreds or thousands. Now if ten people of twenty tell you the same thing, it's probably worth considering. But you're the boss and no one sees the future like you do. In the end, you will be the best judge of what to do.

Use an analytics tool. This tip might not be for everyone. Using analytics tools such as YouTube's built-in analytics or some third-party plugin for your website can take hundreds of hours to derive any benefit. Once you get a good system, however, these tools can trigger feedback immediately. How to use these tools is beyond the scope of this book, so use something like LinkedIn Learning or Lynda.com to learn more about internet analytics. I will add this: I value direct feedback -- anecdotal feedback -- from a real flesh and blood person than I do any analytics tool. Again, it's a balance. If you have only a hundred visitors on your website or video each month, the analytics tool won't tell you much. That one email exchange with a customer is probably better. But if ten thousand visitors all seem to be doing something different than one customer you spoke with, you'll have to make a judgement call. Just know that analytics tools are only as valuable as the person using them.

LEARN YOUR PLATFORM

These tools typically help you track views, promote other videos or products, or monetize (make money). Your audience sees one side of the platform and you, as a publisher, might see another. If you're venturing into a new platform or even a new format -- live streams for example -- then I recommend spending time learning this new area. Audiences can be fickle about new channels that don't seem to "get" how the platform works. And learning a new platform doesn't include only tools and buttons and things like that. It also includes etiquette. Each platform has a different vibe, sort of like music clubs in a city. Follow a few channels for a week or so to get the idea before investing too much in a platform.

LEARN YOUR AUDIENCE

This combines the platform and feedback tips mentioned above. Your audience is not a number. It is a collection of individuals, each with his or her own ideas, sense of humor, and goals. This is why I stress communicating with your audience members as directly as possible, especially in the beginning. You will be surprised at the diversity in your members no matter how niche you think you are. Offer opportunities for your audience to chat with you or send you an email. If you use social media a lot (unlike me), respond to their comments, even if the comment is just "Wow looks good!". If a member leaves a hint as to the other websites or communities she's a part of, check out those as well. Books and video courses try to tell you the "best practices" for getting this information, but none of them amount to much more than I just described in the paragraphs above. The truth is that it is hard work and different for everyone. It's basically a sales job and there's no magic formula for sales.

BUILD PARTNERSHIPS

This tip is a little uncomfortable for most video producers, myself included, but when executed well, it can be very powerful. Get to know other content producers or channels somewhat related to your market. If you create a good relationship with someone who already has a small user base, then ask if you can introduce yourself on his channel. This works primarily if you have a channel driven by a personality or a topic rather than a specific product or service you're trying to promote, at least as far as promoting a video for that product is concerned.

The point is to get your thinking about how your video content fits within a larger community and not only your viewers. Don't think of other channels as "competitors". Instead, they are alliances waiting for your approach. Obviously, this doesn't always work, but the attitude of alliance building will do you well.

INVENT YOUR OWN STRATEGY

This is one of the hardest tips to practice. What works for someone else might not work for you. Keep a journal of your promotion strategy and judge how it's working and what you can improve. There is no magic playbook to get you millions of views in a few weeks or even a few months. Your brain should hurt after you've spent twenty minutes reviewing your strategy and coming up with new ideas. You should feel like you're taking a bit of a risk with each new strategy you want to try. These risks are mostly imaginary and should not include spending money you don't have.

Here are some ideas that I tried:

Find online groups: This strategy works best for channels and free stuff rather than products to sell. Start reading forums and chat channels for your topic. You'll likely try many before keeping a few that mesh with you. Sign up. Read the posts. Respond to a few. Be a quiet but somewhat visible member. After a few weeks, try posting some of your work. See how people react. Don't get discouraged if the reactions are insulting or if they ignore. This will happen to 95% of your efforts. Just gradually post more work and get the occasional good feedback. All the usual destinations are fair game: Facebook groups, Slack channels, Reddit communities. But the best ones are unique and niche, typically hosted on an independent website.

Talk to 5 new people a day: Doing this will serve you well in just about any endeavor. Try to reach out to a new person relevant to your goals each day. When I actually pursue this strategy, it's amazing the information and progress I make. So long as the person is a new connection and even vaguely related to what you're doing, it counts. It's a lot harder than you think. So start with 1 new person and increase from there.

One call to action: You get one shot at asking something from your audience. They can either click your "Subscribe" button, or visit your website, or watch your next video, but they'll rarely do more than one thing, if any. Decide on your most important goal and add that to your video content and somewhere in your descriptions, if applicable. Try that "ask" for a few weeks. Then try another. It's a slow process, but if you're deliberate, you can add your energy to what works.

BEWARE OF PLACING ADS

Ads can help, but are difficult to manage and quickly get expensive. You would need a book as detailed as this one just to get comfortable with the basics. Some services, like Wix, claim to help you publish your ads on networks like Facebook. But just know: getting ads onto Facebook or Google is easy. They just want your money. Getting your ads to be useful is hard work. I spent about $500 on ads -- which is peanuts -- and sold exactly ZERO new books from it.

In my experience, ads have done well for me in cheap spaces. Amazon used to have cheap ad space and it helped me grow. Unfortunately the good times are gone there, especially for Amazon products, so I have to seek greener pastures. But the method perseveres. Find places with good communities and cheap ad space. Local stuff works too. I've placed ads in local magazines and received a better return on investment than with the big online ad tools.

BE PATIENT

I'm an impatient person, so this is the hardest tip for me to follow, but it's also probably the most useful. If you consistently promote *good* content and share your videos with new people, you will gain viewers and followers. The *good* content part is important.

MY ONLY DON'TS

For most rules in video editing, there will be an exception. The following are the only rules I can think of that don't have exceptions. I call this chapter "My Only Don'ts" and not "*The Only Don'ts*" because this is purely my (professional) opinion.

PEAKING AUDIO SHOULD BE A FELONY

Peaking audio or *clipping* audio is enemy number one and punishable by cringing. Nothing destroys a moment more than audio that sounds like it came from a nuclear war zone. What is peaking audio? Peaking audio is distortion caused by audio that is too loud. Peaking audio sounds crackly and noisy. On the timeline below are examples of peaking audio:

The long blue rectangle above depicts a waveform. As you can see, the peaks hit the top of the audio clip which means the audio has peaked. At the right of illustration is the gain meter. The red at the top also means the audio has peaked.

If the audio peaks and distorts because of the way it was recorded then there is no way to fix the sound quality. If the audio sounds fine by itself, but peaks in the timeline, the editor can adjust it. Sometimes the audio peaks because too many loud audio clips have been layered.

If too many audio clips have been layered the editor will have to perform a process called *mixing*. Mixing is the combining of several different sounds or channels into fewer channels or one single channel. Mixing is an entire subject unto itself but here is a simple and fast solution:

1. **Adjust the *gain*.** Most editing programs allow the editor to adjust the *gain* (or volume) of individual audio clips. Bring the gain down or into the negative numbers until the timeline audio sounds normal and the mixer gauge no longer shows red. The gain can be adjusted for one clip or several clips. If only one part is too loud, the part can be cut out and the gain decreased for that particular section. The addition of an audio fade to each cut makes for a seamless transition. Like this:

Normalize before gain: Adjusting the audio by the gain alone is not a good long-term strategy. But as a quick fix for a novice editor or an editor with little time it is a useful technique.

I suggest using the "Normalize" method listed below before using the "Gain" option. Normalizing is just a way of bringing your loudest parts to a specific level. Start with -6db and adjust from there.

2. Use a compressor or limiter. Compressors and limiters are effects which you can add to audio to control the volume dynamically. An editor can search for the "compressor" or "limiter" feature in the software of choice and learn how to use them for individual audio clips, the mixer or the timeline. While this technique is not a perfect solution, it will reduce the most annoying sound distortions.

3. Use a submix. The use of a submix is more advanced than the other sound reduction methods we have discussed. Submixing has the advantage of giving the editor the most flexibility in editing a sound track. Also submixing is considered the most professional technique of the three we have discussed. This is definitely one of those topics where I suggest you watch the video provided from the link.

FLASH FRAMES ARE LITTLE DEVILS

Flash frames are pieces of video or audio and are usually no more than a frame or two in measure. Flash frames occur accidentally: when snapping is turned off or when the clip snaps to the wrong part. Sometimes misaligned layering and incomplete deletes cause flash frames.

Flash frames don't happen often, and experienced editors usually catch them quickly. Nevertheless, good editors watch for them as they finalize their finished projects. A friend of mine had just finished editing a draft of a feature documentary that premiered at a popular festival. He and I were watching the documentary together in the theater with an audience of over one hundred when he noticed a flash frame. He was embarrassed even though I doubt less than a few people in the audience noticed the mistake.

To fix these gaps, just move the video over or extend one or both of the clips until the gap is filled. Watch your video on the biggest screen you can and ask others to watch it with you.

APPENDIX: RESOURCES

Consider these as starting points. During your research on a project, expect to find solutions and products that help you even more than the ones I recommend. Some of these resources might be considered "advanced," so don't get discouraged or overwhelmed if some of this information is not immediately useful or comprehensible.

SERVICES AND PRODUCTS FOR LEARNING EDITING SOFTWARE

- LinkedIn Learning (formerly Lynda.com): The best paid instructional service. Thousands of videos on video editing, production, and just about anything else you can think of. Some libraries provide you with a free Lynda account, so check your local branch.

- VideoCopilot.net: This is mostly an effects resource, but the host and creator, Andrew Kramer, is very smart, funny, and thorough. He will give you an idea of how to *think* visually and problem solve. The tutorials are not as up-to-date as other resources these days, but Andrew's approach to effects is timeless.

- CreativeCow.net: Useful forums for finding and asking questions regarding most creative tasks, including video editing.

- Adobe's Help Forums: https://helpx.adobe.com These can be a little tough to learn from, but they provide the most complete and up-to-date information for Adobe products. I use them a lot.

- YouTube: I know it's probably obvious for many of you, but I wanted to include it just in case. Couple of tips though:

Watch more than one video on a certain topic or tool. Some explanations are more complete than others. Nothing is more frustrating than following a tutorial to find halfway through that the lesson doesn't apply to your project. I usually skip to the middle and end to make sure the video doesn't go a direction I don't need.

If you're searching for program-specific features, make sure the video is not more than a year or two old. All of this software changes quickly now and many tutorials go out of date, especially for errors and problems.

Advanced editing software
- Adobe Creative Cloud - Premiere Pro $30-50 per month.

- Apple - FinalCut Pro X (or FinalCut Pro 7 if you can get it): $300 one-time payment

- Davinci - Resolve - $300 (you have to buy this through a re-seller, such as B&H or Amazon).

Beginner editing software
- Premiere Rush - $20 per month

- WeVideo.com: $4-30 per month

- Filmora.Wondershare.com: $40-80 per year.

- YouTube - Creator Studio Video Editor: Free

- Apple - iMovie: Free with most Macs. Otherwise $15 on Apple Store

- Windows - MovieMaker: Free with Windows

Compressors and encoders

- Squared5 - MpegStream Clip

- Handbrake (open source)

- Apple - Compressor

- Adobe - Media Encoder

Storage and delivery

Amazon Drive: Free for 5 Gigs, then $2-7 for up to a terabyte per a month. For advanced users with waaaay more data, check out their S3 and Glacier storage services (note, these are very advanced services compared to Drive).

- Google Drive: $0, 5, 10 per month

- DropBox: $0 or about $10 per month

- WireDrive: $300+ per month

- WeTransfer: $0 or about $10 per month

- Hightail: $0 or about $12 per month

- Wipster.io: $25 and up per month

Hosting and sharing

- YouTube: Free

- Vimeo: $0, 5, or 17 per month

- Facebook: Free

- Instagram: Free

- SnapChat: Free

- Bitchute: Free (and donation memberships)

- Dailymotion: Free

- Rumble: Free

Effects

- Videohive.net: Also known as the Envato Market, you can buy pre-made graphics and video. You can even hire others for tasks too difficult or time-consuming for yourself.

- FilmImpact.net: *Transition Pack 1*. Works for Premiere Pro only. As I write this, part of this pack is free to install. But it'll be worth the price for the video transitions. They are much better than the built-in transitions Premiere provides.

- VideoBlocks.com: Lots of interesting textures, videos and graphics to filter/layer over/under your clips and titles.

Royalty-free music

- YouTube - Creator Studio Audio/Music Library: Free (this is mostly what I use)

- PremiumBeat.com: $50-200 per track

- EpidemicSound.com: Decent selection of music. Used by a lot of digital agencies.

Raw and Ultra HD Support

- Premiere Pro, Final Cut Pro X and iMovie all support 4K video (but the format support varies).

Premiere Pro supports Raw and Ultra HD camera formats from Canon, Phantom, RED, and SONY (and is constantly being updated to more).

Be sure you are familiar with *proxies* before using 4K and most raw files.

Although Adobe and Apple (and other editing program creators) are good about updating the software for current camera format compatibility, you still might need to download/install camera format **codecs** and plugins from the camera manufacturer's website (i.e., SONY, Canon). The website links are always changing, but the downloads you need are usually under "Drivers and Downloads" or something like that.

General cinema theory

- *In the Blink of an Eye*: By editor Walter Murch. It's the best general film editing theory book I've read.

- *Every Frame a Painting*: By editor Tony Zhou. He makes video essays on movies and often approaches them from an editor's perspective. You can find his channel by searching the name on YouTube.

Resources for general video production

- VideoCopilot.net: As mentioned above, it's mostly a visual effects tutorial site. But sometimes Andrew and his team show you their shooting methods, which can be quite helpful.

- FilmRiot: FilmRiot is a popular YouTube channel for general video production. They are not as funny as Andrew Kramer (though they try hard to be) but have excellent tutorials on development, production and post production: https://www.youtube.com/user/filmriot

GLOSSARY

Arrow: A tool in the video editing software. Mostly, you'll be click-dragging clips with it and right-clicking to get additional options.

Aspect Ratio: The shape of the video screen (or captured camera video). Common ratio include 4:3 and 16:9.

Audience: The targeted viewers for your video. The intended audience should greatly influence how you make decisions.

B-roll: Supplemental video and clips to use over (or between) your main (or most important) video.

Bins: The organizational folders within the project panel of your editing software.

Bit rate: The number of bits transferred in a given amount of time such as 1 kilobit per second (1 kbit/s) or 40 megabits per second (40 MB/s)

Blend Modes: The method by which images are layered together. This is an option in your effects panel of your editing software.

Bit and bytes: These are units of digital information. Eight bits usually make a byte.

Codecs: A device or program used to encode or decode data streams (like video and audio).

Color Correcting/Grading: The process of changing the color of video to achieve a certain look.

Community: The collection of people active on platforms, like the YouTube community or Reddit community.

Compression: The process of making a file smaller.

Content: The things that happen in the video, like someone talking, a car zooming by, a tree shaking from wind.

Cut-aways: Similar to B-roll: video clips you layer on top of your main video track.

Cut/Blade/Slice/Razor: A tool in your editing software. You use it to divide a video or audio clip.

Definition: Similar to resolution; it's the amount of pixels within a video frame (or aspect ratio).

Delivering/Sharing: The method or technology you use to send your videos for instant playback.

Dissolve/Fade: A transition. The gradual removal of one clip to reveal the next.

DSLR: Digital Single-lens Reflex camera. These cameras look like still-photography cameras but also shoot video. They are very popular among amateur and professional videographers.

Editor: The person in charge of assembling all of the media into its final form.

Effects: Any visual or audio element added to the source video.

Encoding (analog to digital): The process of copying a video into a different format.

Export: The process of turning your editing software timeline/sequence into a single video format/file.

File format: The collection of data that makes your video, like the video, audio, and metadata.

Flash Frame: One or more (but usually fewer than 10) video frames unintentionally left in a video.

Folders: The organizational structure of your computer, like your Documents folder or your Applications folder.

Frames: The individual images that make your video.

Frame rate: The amount of frames in a given time. Common rates include 24 frames per second (24 fps), 29.97 (or 30) fps, or 59.94 (or 60) fps.

Gain: The overall adjustment of the volume of your audio.

Graphics Card: Hardware in your computer that feeds the video to your monitor. An important piece for video editing.

Hosting: A service for storing data (and sometimes delivering) data.

Impact (Style 2): The editing style where the edits themselves drive the rhythm and pacing of the video.

Import: The process of adding media to your editing project/software.

In/Out: Where a clip begins and ends.

Keyframes: Set points that change video or audio effects.

Layering (Decision 2): The process of organizing clips on more than one track.

Layers: Could also be synonymous with "tracks." They are the stacks of video or audio in your timeline.

Layout: How your editing software is organized or how the elements within your program monitor are composed.

Level (audio): Similar to gain in that it shows the volume of audio, but is dynamic. Meaning, your audio levels are the high and low points (the waveform) of your audio.

Markers: Points you set in your video or audio. You can also add notes to your markers.

Media: All of the video, audio, and image content for your projects.

Media Browser: The panel in your editing software that allows you to view and import media from your computer or hard drives.

Media Cache: The folder where your editing software stores data.

Metadata: Information that accompanies your video, audio or image files, such as date, resolution or location.

Micro editing: Editing on the frame-by-frame level of the timeline.

Music Montage/ Music Video (Format 1): The process of editing to the music rather than to the content within the video.

Natural Hit: A moment of collision or impact within a video, like a bat hitting a ball, a person snapping his finger, or a blink of an eye.

Omitting (Decision 4): The tough decision of what to leave out of your timeline.

On camera: When a subject is visible in the video instead of just heard (off camera).

Online storage: A service that stores your data via uploading to the Internet, like DropBox or Google Drive.

Opacity: How visible your video is on a layer. 0 is invisible, 100 is completely visible.

Past Self/Present Self: The editor you were before, the editor you are now.

Peaking/Clipping Audio: Audio that is too loud for the capture or playback device.

Pixels: The smallest element of your video image. 1920x1080 means 1,920 pixels by 1,080 pixels.

Platform: The website or environment where your video or content will be displayed, like YouTube, Facebook, or the projector in your conference room.

Playhead: The icon or line in your timeline or source monitor that indicates where you are in a video or audio piece.

Processor: The part of your computer that does most of the data manipulation.

Producer: The person in charge on a video project of making sure everything gets done. Sometimes the producer is responsible for creative and distribution decisions as well.

Program Monitor: The panel in your editing software that displays your edits in the timeline.

Project Panel: The panel in your editing software that displays all of your imported media.

Proxy: A smaller version of a big video, usually a video too big to play properly on your computer.

Push: A video transition where one clip moves out of frame as another clip enters.

RAM: Random Access Memory. The parts of your computer that store temporary data.

Raw: Video and audio that received no processing or compressing.

Reel: An edited video displaying your skills as an editor (or anything else for that matter).

Runtime: The length (in seconds, minutes or hours) of a video.

Screen Real Estate: The amount of space on screen you have available to compose within.

Scrubbing: Quickly reviewing media by dragging the playhead across the timeline (either in the timeline panel or source monitor) or by watching the media at twice the speed.

Selects: Isolated, trimmed clips from the media, but not edited enough to be considered a draft. Usually several takes or alternatives are included within a selects sequence.

Self storage: Home hard drives or servers.

Sequences: timelines that hold your edited videos

Side-by-Side (Decision 1): When two clips sit next to each other (without a space between) on the timeline.

Snapping: The feature in editing software that automatically aligns clips and other media with the in and out points and markers.

Source Monitor: The panel in your editing software where you can review your media.

Stealth (Style 1): The "traditional" style of editing. The goal is to make the editing unnoticeable.

Style: The pacing, tone and look of your video.

Stylist: A pen and tablet or monitor. A useful tool for digital drawing and editing.

Take(s): The numbering system used in recording a scene, usually from a scripted piece (like a movie or tutorial).

The Scene (Format 2): Usually a scripted piece (like a movie or TV show) that includes dialog or planned actions.

Timecode: The system used to record the hours, minutes, seconds, and frames of media.

timeline: The panel in your editing software where all of your edits go.

Timing (Decision 3): The decision of when to place a certain clip or clips.

Titles/Overlays: Text, graphics and images that play on layers/tracks above your video clips.

Tools: The panel in your editing software that shows cursor states such as the arrow, hand and razor.

Track: The stacks of video and audio streams on your timeline.

Transcoding (digital to digital): The process of copying a digital file into a new format.

Transitions: The effects used from switching one clip to another.

Unlinking: The process of separating joined video and audio.

Version Control (versioning): The process of frequently saving new versions of your sequences or projects.

Vlog: Video Weblog (or blog). A category of video where the creator talks to the audience directly.

Voice over and the VO Montage (Format 3): Voice over is when a person's voice plays along with video that is not of the speaker (at least, not of the speaker as he/she is speaking). The Voice-over Montage is a common format where the voice over audio provides the most drive and information of the video.

Zoom: The process of scaling the video to a specific point within the frame.

ACKNOWLEDGEMENTS

I'd like to thank...

My good friend and fellow video renegade Lee Iovino at the Seattle Science Foundation. Without him I probably would've learned filmmaking the polite way. Lame.

Tal Levitas at OutPostVFX for filling in many of my technology and business gaps, especially during the early editions of the book. He's living proof that the saying "you can't know it all" is wrong.

Geoff Yano at Disney Digital for providing me with many organizational and resource ideas. I've since upgraded my process as a result of interviewing him for the original publication book.

Cheryl Campsmith, editor of Gortimer Gibbon's, for her enlightening interview about a career as a Hollywood editor. She helped me realize just how hard we all have to work.

My parents, Art and Mary Lou, for their generous support both during the shaky moments in my career and for being the first to review and edit drafts of original and subsequent versions of this book.

My wife, Mary, for her encouragement and guidance in all my endeavors as well as her help with the original design and editing of this book.

Lastly, thank you, dear reader and editor, for taking time out of your day to learn from this book. I promise to update this with the best information and ideas whenever possible.

ABOUT THE AUTHOR

I'm Aaron Goold. I wrote, directed, and, yes, edited the science fiction movie *Immersion: A Metaphysical Wandering*, available if you search hard enough. I have edited hundreds (possibly thousands) of videos for companies such as Disney Digital, Warner Bros. Studios, Machinima, America's Funniest Home Videos, and StyleHaul. Currently, Other publications of mine include the audio story series *The Hidden Pages* -- check it out at thehiddenpages.net -- and various collections of music.

Printed in Great Britain
by Amazon

61151198R00077